My Will Be Done

Sheri H. Thrower

Copyright © 2016 SHERI H. THROWER All rights reserved. This book or any portion thereof may not be reproduced or used in any manner whatsoever without the express written permission of the publisher except for the use of brief quotations in a book review.

Limits of Liability and Disclaimer of Warranty

The author and publisher shall not be liable for your misuse of this material. This book is strictly for informational and educational purposes.

The purpose of this book is to educate and entertain. The author and/or publisher do not guarantee that anyone following these techniques, suggestions, tips, ideas, or strategies will become successful. The author and/or publisher shall have neither liability nor responsibility to anyone with respect to any loss or damage caused, or alleged to be caused, directly or indirectly by the information contained in this book.

Although the author and publisher have made every effort to ensure that the information in this book was correct at press time, the author and publisher do not assume and hereby disclaim any liability to any party for any loss, damage, or disruption caused by errors or omissions, whether such errors or omissions result from negligence, accident, or any other cause. Views expressed in this publication do not necessarily reflect the views of the publisher.

      Printed in the United States of America
 ISBN 978-0692629574
STM Publishing Chattanooga, TN 37411
Editor: Jeffrey P. Duke
Cover: Averi Thrower and Emily Thompson

Dedication

This book is lovingly dedicated to my Dad and Mom, Rev. G. David and Charlotte Henderson. Not only have they taught me the meaning of sacrificial living, they have demonstrated it throughout their lives and daily service to others, and to each other. As my Dad always reminds me:

God never promises to speak twice to us. Hear what He says the first time and obey. Obedience is the key to blessing.

I can only hope to be half as obedient in my life and ministry as he and my mom have been. If there were ever two mortals who lived the words of our family song, "Not my will, but Thine be done," it would be them. I pray that my ambitions and plans align with the heart of God in the way I have seen theirs do over my lifetime; but God has a unique path for each one of us called to His purposes. "Lord, form in me a heart of obedience."

Mom and Dad—they love God; they love people. I am thankful that I am one of those people.

Sheri H. Thrower

Acknowledgments

  I have to admit that I am not completely "there" when it comes to giving of my will in every area of my life. I have not arrived—as it were—but the journey is thrilling. And writing this book has helped me become more trusting of Jesus daily; at times, minute by minute. "Oh for grace to trust Him more."

  I am not sure "easy" is a word I would use to describe viewing his altar of sacrifice. It is not easy to sacrifice everything we love to conclude, "Here, God. You take it. If it dies, so be it. But if You give it back, give it back with everlasting life and power, honoring Your name." It is worthy sacrificing that which brings Him honor. I am learning to be done with those things that He deems unworthy of my focus. I will always be learning to be done. He will always be my Teacher.

  I would like to thank my family for understanding my "writing zone" and for their patience while I linger in it for a few months. Thank you, Averi, Michael, Mom, Dad, and Pippy! You are the best. And to my daughter, Averi Thrower, whose thoughts on girls her age "being done," which inspired the title and theme of this book. Being done is ageless.

  And to my editor, Jeffrey P. Duke: thank you for taking aim but not shooting your laptop during times of revision and correction of these inspirations! It means much to have an editor who is in one accord theologically and spiritually with each word written and considered. Thank you for making me think, re-consider and re-write to the best of my ability. And thank you for helping me to remember that "Help me Jesus" is still the best, most honest, needed prayer. Always.

  To Ann Downing and the wonderful ladies of Middle Tennessee Women's Retreat (MTWR). Thank you for another

My Will be Done

opportunity to speak and lead worship, teaching the truths in God's Word. You have groomed me as a speaker, singer, worshipper and now, author. I am thankful that God still uses us to honor Him in the same setting: hotel banquet halls and chocolate cake served tables. I love each one of you.

   To Emily Thompson and my daughter, Averi Thrower. Thank you for a wonderful cover and graphic art design. Amazing! I love you both.

   To each reader, thank you for taking the time to read my thoughts in written word. If not for you, I have no reason to click the keys and share my crazy stories and life. I appreciate you so much.

   To my Heavenly Father, thank You for holding my hand on this journey of accepting Your will for my life. Your pen, Your eraser. Daily.

Blessings,
Sheri

Sheri H. Thrower

Preface

I use the word, "people" below because my thoughts are human thoughts to human creatures. But in fairness, because I am a woman, my sentiments come from the female perspective and are directed to women, who—by the way—make up the majority of audiences to whom I speak.

This book is for the steel-willed people in the world—for those "London Bridge" souls, who, when they fall, always rebuild. The tragedy is that they frequently rebuild on the same shaky foundations from which they fell. And still, their hope is to find the strength and will to rebuild. So it is, with jaws firmly set, teeth tightly clinched, that their ironclad determinations withstand the warning signs of life, friends, family, and yes, even Heaven itself. Their spirits resonate with the lyrics, "iron bars won't bend and break. Iron bars won't bend and break, my fair lady."

This book is written for the "unbreakable people," who… have been broken.

But to remain in brokenness, itself, is to declare defeat. So, I write to people whose wills have been melted by the very breath of heaven that redirects us. I write to those who have stood nose to nose with their Creator, daring Him to interrupt their self-inflicted ways, while hoping that He does just that.

This book is written to encourage the down-trodden that through tears of sorrow there can be tears of joy together with the revelation that He is in fact a God of boundaries. And we become thankful for the line that He has drawn.

For the line is sacred. It is where His will begins. And ours is done. This book is for those who no longer wish to "kick" the line, but long to gaze with expectation at His perfect plan.

My Will be Done

Lord…
Your pen,
Your eternal ink,
Your eraser,
Every day.

Contents

1 DONE HANDING GOD THE MOP 1

2 DONE WITH THE WEIGHT 5

3 DONE WITH GUAVA POPSICLES 15

4 DONE EXPECTING SMOOTH 19

5 DONE BEING GOMER 23

6 DONE WITH NORMAL 29

7 DONE NOT APPRECIATING MY INFLUENCE 33

8 DONE BEING GOOD 39

9 DONE BEING HOLY SPIRT, JR. 45

10 DONE WITH STOOPING 51

11 DONE WITH LA LA LAND 53

12 DONE WITH INSECURITY'S VOICE 57

13 DONE WITH THE EXPIRATION DATE 61

14 DONE WITH ALZHEIMER'S FAITH 65

15 DONE NOT CALLING IT WHAT IT IS 71

16 DONE SLEEPING WITH THE ENEMY 75

17 DONE WITH HUNGER GAMES 79

18 DONE WITH THE PEN 85

19 DONE NOT RESTING 89

20 DONE BEING HACKED 93

21 DONE WITH ENVY 97

22 DONE WITH WRESTLING 103

23 DONE WITH WHITE KNUCKLES 107

24 DONE WITH GREASED POLE THEOLOGY 113

25 WELL, DONE 117

1 DONE HANDING GOD THE MOP

My Mom says I was nearly a year old when she sat me in my high chair and placed scrambled eggs in front of me for the first time. We were visiting my Granny Henderson's—Wimple Cordelia Henderson. I was expecting Cheerios but was offered a rubbery yellow glob of protein. The eggs were healthy, good for me, but there was a problem: I did not like scrambled eggs…at all—not the way they looked, smelled and certainly not the way the regurgitated looking goo felt between my chubby little fingers. My mother tells me I decided to put an end to that trial.

She says I poked at my scrambled eggs and pinched off little pieces, one at a time. I raised each little chunk in the air and stared in awe at it. I held it to my nose, made a sour face and placed it gingerly back on my plate. Then, as though no one could see what I was doing, I picked up a bunch at once, looked at my mother with my wrinkled nose, grinned like a Cheshire cat and dangled them over the edge of my highchair tray. One by one, gravity got the best of each morsel as it was dropped to the floor. I thought no one was the wiser. And so, I continued this charade until my plate was empty. The yellow contrast must have been spectacular on the brown linoleum squares. And after the entire serving had been transferred from my plate to the floor, I dusted my hands clean, wiped my mouth, and pretended I had cleared my entire plate. How proud I must have looked?

My grandmother observed the entire performance. She grinned as she watched me transfer my entire meal onto her floor. And just as my Mom was about to smack my hands for making the mess, my grandmother whispered to her, "Just let her finish…let her finish. Let her finish her mess." And that is what my mother did: allowed me to create a "messy mess" all over my Granny Henderson's floor. They looked on with amusement

My Will be Done

because they both knew what was in store for me. And what happened next is likely the reason that, still today, I dread hearing the words, "Let's clean up the kitchen."

Mom strolled over to my high chair, gently untied my bib, pulled out my sticky wooden egg covered tray, lifted me out of the chair and calmly said, "Ok. All done? Good! It's time to clean up your mess now!"

Mom seemed thrilled with our little party. I was, evidently, unimpressed. But I tiptoed through the yellowy mess, picking up every morsel. Once finished, I went to my grandmother's arms expecting to be consoled for such a "harsh punishment."

I cleaned up my own disaster and I never dropped eggs on a floor again. My mother then cleaned *me*.

I see now that in walking the Christian road, God is a lot like my Mom. We all make messes. And God gives us the space and freedom to make 'em. We often discard what is intended for our good. At times, we toss to the floor what is healthy. And when we are no longer enamored with what God puts on our plate, we give Him the Cheshire cat grin and simply do as we wish. We ignore his way and give full liberty to our own wills. Then, unashamedly we smile at God as if He cannot see what we've been up to. But He waits. And in his providence and time He comes to us and says, "Ok. All done? Good. Time to clean up." The discipline, born of purest love, comes. And in that love, He goes hand in hand with us. But the clean-up must still be done.

Just the other day, I asked Mom about this story. I had heard it before but the details were sketchy. And while originally writing this chapter, I wondered if I had kicked and cried during the discipline like any normal toddler would. I wanted to be able to say that that is exactly how I responded, but to my surprise, she explained that the opposite was true. "No. You did not kick and scream or cry. You were always an obedient child, so when

I asked you to pick up your mess, you simply did it; no questions asked, no fussing or whining. You just did what you were told."

After my Mom enlightened me, I could just see God in heaven, slapping his knee, throwing His head back in laughter and saying, "Where did *that* little girl go?" And I wondered to myself, "I did? My, how things change!"

Do messes keep showing up in your life? If so, do you kick, scream and blame everyone including God for them? We do everything *but* take responsibility. We behave like teenagers in a hotel room on Spring Break for the first time. We trash the place, then leave it all for the maid to clean. "Here, God. You clean it up!"

All through Scripture we read how God charges His people to take action when they have followed their own ways rather than His. He wants nothing different for us; to mop up our own hurtful words, to clean up the aftermath of lost tempers and piercing verbal assaults.

Jesus does not go to those we have wounded to say, "Hey, you know Sheri really is sorry for what she said. And she sent me to apologize. So, if you will give her just one more chance, I am certain she won't do that again. Besides, you know how we all make mistakes, right? So, if you'll just step to the side, I'm going to mop up this little mess she made in your life."

No, He places the responsibility for our messes squarely on our plates:

[23]*"Therefore, if you are offering your gift at the altar and there remember that your brother or sister has something against you,* [24]*leave your gift there in front of the altar. First go and be reconciled to them; then come and offer your gift."* Matt. 5:23, 24 (NIV)

Note that the revelation at the altar is not of another's wrong to us, but a remembrance that another may have something against us because of *our* hurtful words or actions against them!

My Will be Done

God hands us the mop of reconciliation and says, "Clean."

He charges us with four actions once the Holy Spirit delivers the conviction:
1. Leave…your self-will and pride.
2. Go…make the effort.
3. Reconcile…ask the difficult question, "Will you forgive me?"
4. *Then* come.

We usually do it all downright backwards. We realize what we've done and then we go to Jesus. The problem is, we get stuck there. We know that in Jesus the Father will forgive us, especially if "we promise not to do it again." But we can remain in that "spiritually retarded" state for years, just to avoid any action. Clean up is not easy nor pain-free. We need to stop putting it off. Let us go, clean up the floor and then breathe in the miraculous work God completes once we have done our part.

Parents, none of us has done it perfectly. Surely, you—like me—have made numerous parenting blunders. Your children need your healing apologies. Get over your pride. Be reconciled.

Hand God your mop…once you are done with it.

2 DONE WITH THE WEIGHT

Recently, my grandmother gave away her beautiful, antique, mahogany-colored baby grand piano, which had been in our family for decades. I wonder if the new owner has any idea that if given the gift of speech, that piano could tell a thousand stories and memories from my childhood? My grandmother is ninety-five now; that is a lot of stories. But more than memories, that piano endured a lot of plunking around from her children to her great, great grandchildren. Tiny, dirty fingers tapped out notes from "twinkle-twinkle little star" to beethoven's "fur elise."

That piano served our family well over years and years as it accompanied us through many of the greatest songs and hymns ever written. I recall my aunt's long, slender fingers stretching across imperfect octaves, while my dad played along on the Hammond organ across the room, rolling some camp meeting style chords. I hope I never forget his Schroeder-like posture as he played while we sang.

Although the piano was beautiful, it was imperfect. Its most notable flaw, like with many older pieces, was that it was modestly out of tune. And the keys were heavy, if not resistant. Even the most practiced hands were weary after a few tunes on the old girl; the weighted ivory favored slower ballads.

Despite these innate imperfections, we still sang from our hearts and through our souls. One hymn I recall in particular was my Dad's favorite; we called it "our family song" though its real title is "Not My Will." The lyrics were penned by Arthur Smith:

My Will be Done

> *If I ask for things that I should not ask for*
> *If I pray for things selfishly*
> *If I ask for myself and not for my neighbor*
> *Lift this veil from my eyes, let me see*
> *Chorus:*
> *Not My Will, Thine Be Done*
> *Prayed Jesus*
> *May this same prayer be mine every day.*
> *When this robe of flesh that I wear makes me falter*
> *Guide my steps*
> *Hold my hand all the way.*

God knows that as much as I love these lyrics, they still cause me pain when I sing them today. Even as I type these words now, my heart stumbles. Like those "heavy" piano keys, the message embodied in the lyrics weighs me down. Why? Because I'm reminded of the war that continues to rage inside me: my way versus my Heavenly Father's. And my "robe of flesh" persistently "blows the class curve" at my faltering.

If I put a check beside each verse that convicts me, I must start line one: "If I ask for things that I should not ask for...." Check. I've asked for a multitude of things that serve my will.

Do "I pray for things selfishly?" Check. Rinse and repeat.

Do "I ask for myself and not my neighbor?" Scoring one hundred thus far. I might recall my neighbor once in a blue moon. I'm not overly acquainted with selflessness; let's leave it at that.

Just for fun, I asked *Siri* on my cell phone today, "What does 'faltering' mean?" She answered: "Faltering means to lose strength or momentum." If you are anything like me, you have noticed that what we lose when faltering, are generally the most valuable weapons for living the Christian life: we need strength to resist spiritual darkness and momentum in faith to persevere.

Because we are image bearers, we know God has a sense of humor. He must be amused as He watches how strong we start out in the race of pursuing what we think will make us happy. Like a runner on our mark, the gun of self-desire explodes, and we're off! Some of us run for years pursuing self-indulgence only to find that the satisfaction was fleeting, and soon forgotten. Others learn quickly from their mistakes and turn to go a different, better way.

But those of us who are stubborn, learn life the hard way and carry the weight of regret. We don't consider how heavy regret would be when we look around at the people who have been hurt by our wrong choices. We forget about the chasm that will exist between us and God after finally getting our way. We don't realize there will be powerlessness in our prayer life. We totally missed that one, forgetting that *the effectual, fervent prayer of a righteous man avails much.* (James 5:16) Or, "the diligent prayer of a righteous person, has great effect." And it is under the weight of regret that we throw ourselves to the ground-prostrate before Him. Out of breath and exhausted from the fun, we lie on our backs and ponder every "if only" in our lives:

> "If only I had never taken that first drink."
> "If only I had never clicked on the website."
> "If only I had never agreed to meet with him or her alone."
> "If only I had not gone along with the crowd."
> "If only I had asked God for help in showing me the way out."

The life of the wealthiest king of all time—King Solomon—is instructive. Like a lot of us, he learned the hard way. Listen to what he says about getting his way: *"Whatever my eyes desired I did not keep from them...then I looked on the works my hands had done...and indeed all was vanity and grasping for the wind."* Ecclesiastes 2:19-11 (NKJV). King Solomon speaks volumes in just a few words about his eyes and his hands. He, like many of us, became entangled by what he

My Will be Done

allowed himself to see. Insert here, "Oh Be Careful Little Eyes What You See." There is an abundance of truth in those words. All it takes is a glance in the wrong direction and our feet generally follow where our eyes lead. And though men are frequently stereotyped in this regard, women are not immune...at all. Does Potiphar's wife come to mind?

King Solomon looked upon many women to satisfy his flesh. And though he started out asking God for wisdom, the end result was not what he anticipated. He likely did not expect to find vanity. The "Spirit of King Solomon" falls upon women as well. If we do not keep ourselves from every desire that comes along, we will end up carrying a heavy weight of insecurity and hurt that can take years or a lifetime to overcome. Being a single woman in ministry, I am very aware of the enemy's attacks. Often, we use this as an excuse, however, when we knowingly put ourselves into tempting situations. And when it comes to temptation, whether we are in ministry or not, it is helpful to recall the words in Song of Solomon 8:4: *"I adjure you, O daughters of Jerusalem, that you stir not up, nor awaken love until it pleases."* (ESV) Stirring up love and the passion that accompanies it before its time, can lead to pain that God never intended for us. If you have awakened love and passion in the wrong relationship before its time, stand up, dust yourself off, get back into the Word so that God may renew and help you to do what God has called you to do. I do not want to oversimplify here. Entrenched and habitual sin requires confession, accountability, surrendering our wills, and self-denial. And staying busy is a good thing for single women. If you are married, keep loving and encouraging your spouse. Pray for him so that love remains awakened.

King Solomon's dad knew about faltering and waking up passions too soon. In fact, daddy King David should have let his own "love" continue sleeping during rooftop bathing sessions next to the palace. His feet followed where his eyes were looking and his heart faltered. So much destruction and pain followed his selfish choice here. David knew well about leanness of soul and empty-heartedness. Murder and adultery can be the induction ceremony to both. And if you listen to the tone of his writings in the Psalms, you will hear his pain. Maybe that is why it was easy for him to recall the children of Israel's journey in Psalm 106:15 where wrote, *"(God) gave them their request, but sent leanness into their soul."* Both the children of Israel and David felt the weight of getting their way. It was an empty hearted place

I've known empty hearted places. I, like David, can easily relate to the children of Israel and God sending leanness into my soul. Do you see yourself in that way? We have all posed for a picture perfect scene of disobedience, framed in self-will. The children of Israel are a picture of us, our hearts. God sometimes indulges us with our insistent desires. He allows us to have our way, not to harm but to teach. A commentator of this verse suggests that leanness comes into our souls the very instant God grants us our selfish desire. Having our way and a shallow soul come as a pair.

Personally, I find myself looking for God's baseball bat of correction when I have insisted on my way. Or, I wait for His angry finger to point me to the woodshed of life. But this is a false narrative of who God is. I am probably not alone in working hard to overcome my view of God as an angry judge with a baseball bat, ready to whack me over the head when I do something wrong. There are times when God has told me "No" but I pursued them anyway. And while I believe there are occasions where God "sends us to the wood shed" because of His corrective love, in those times He has allowed me to experience the consequences of my choices. And it is there, in the valley, where I am most humbled and contrite. It is there where I listen, and learn.

My Will be Done

Ask the alcoholic who wearied of having enough rehab certificates to wallpaper the rooms of her house. The struggle is exhausting. The severed relationships and serial job-hopping is too much. For the fortunate ones, change becomes easier than the habit. Pain can bring change. We might expect a severe correction or "punishment" for their sin and its consequences. But God shows up in their lives with the corrective tool of dissatisfaction, and it becomes enough. Dissatisfaction can be from above, a "God thing."

I hear stories from women whose husbands stopped having multiple affairs simply because they got tired of them. It took too much energy to be unfaithful. It takes energy to sin, period. My dad, a minister, describes energy to sin like this. Sin takes energy. And the more we sin, the stronger that sin becomes. It's like going to the gym and working out. If you lift weights, a muscle grows. And if you exercise one arm more than the other, one arm is going to be stronger and bigger. It's the same with sin. What we exercise is what becomes strong in our lives. If we are selfish, it is because we have flexed the muscle of selfish living. If we have problems with sexual sin, it is because we are flexing that muscle by giving into our desires and repeating the sin. If we simply stop flexing the muscle, however, it becomes weaker in our lives. And one "No," to temptation leads to another "No." Once we take the step to resist temptation one time, it becomes easier the next and its muscle weakens. If you want purity, exercise pureness. If you want selfishness to die, exercise generosity daily. Build those muscles you desire to be strong in your life. Stop building sin muscles and make a conscious decision to be "done with it."

David knew all too well about flexing sin's muscle when he faltered with Bathsheba. After being confronted by Nathan the prophet, he admits to God, *"Against you and you only have I sinned and done what is evil in your sight."* David pours out his heart before God and continues with a prayer, "*¹⁰Create in me a pure heart, O God, and renew a steadfast spirit within me. ¹¹Do not cast me from your presence or take your Holy Spirit from me. ¹²Restore to me the joy of your salvation **and grant me a willing spirit,** to sustain me."* (Psalm 51: 10-12; (NIV, emphasis added)

I love the way David asked for God to grant him a willing spirit. Would it not benefit us to do the same? When we need to walk away from unhealthy situations we might utter David's words: "Grant me a willing spirit, O God." When we find it difficult to control our temper: "Grant me a willing spirit, O God." When God calls us to forgive the one who has hurt us most: "Grant me a willing spirit, O God." When the weight of habit and familiarity is stronger than the desire for change: "Grant me a willing spirit, O God."

God is faithful to give us an obedient, willing spirit: "*For it is God who works in you both to will and to do of his good pleasure."* Philippians 2:13 (ESV)

Do you have a sudden change of heart about a habit or sin in your life? That's God working in you to do his good pleasure. Are you bored with familiarity of today and ready to risk tomorrow? That's God working in you to do his good pleasure. Are you finally tired of the weight that self-indulgence offers? That is God. Let him do the work that only He can do.

Done with it? That is God!

Like my grandmother's old piano, God will remove the very things that are a burden or weight to us. Oddly, if not miraculously, we miss the weight because it was nothing but familiar. But all good things come from above and God knows better than we how to provide us with a divine substitution. In my grandmother's living room sits a new piano now. Its ivories are easier to play and its wood even more beautiful. And that is a picture of what God will do in us. In you.

My Will be Done

I am thankful for our family song.
 Living the weight of my will has naturally made me more accepting of His.
I'm done with the weight.
How about you?
That's God.

Sheri H. Thrower

Be done thinking your prayers
fall to the ground.
They rise like incense to His throne.

Psalm 141:2 *"May my prayer be set before you like incense, may the lifting of my hands be like an evening sacrifice." (NIV)*

My Will be Done

DONE

3 DONE WITH GUAVA POPSICLES

I have a new idea for a crash diet. Add guava fruit to your diet, include "sulfur drinking water" from south florida and, voila! You are sure to shed a number of pounds!

My first experience with what I call, "the detestable taste of guava fruit," was when I visited Dad's family in South Florida as a child. My grandfather pastored a church in Moore Haven and one of his congregants invited my family over for an afternoon refresher: guava popsicles. I was five at the time and remember being so hungry, anticipating the yumminess of the homemade ice cream on a sweltering hot Florida day. We all gathered on the front porch to eat and my mother handed me my frozen treat on its tan wooden stick. I sunk my teeth into the thick, rich iciness and all I remember was that my face puckered uncontrollably, contorting into what must have looked like the main character in a horror flick. I embarrassed my mother by letting my disdain show. While she wasn't looking, I threw the rest of my frozen treat into the shrubs behind me, hoping that my taste buds and guava would never meet again.

I wish that strongholds in my life would become like guava fruit to my soul? Oh for the day that addictions and strongholds would finally cause our best horror faces to appear, as we grow sick of their claws in our lives. How relieved we would be if the taste of sin finally sickened us.

Well, what if I told you that it is possible with a "prayer of blessing?" God's word tells us that in John 8:32, *"And ye shall know the truth and the truth shall set you free."*(KJV) When we pray for God's blessing over our lives and those whom we love, we are asking Him to send truth. We tend to think that blessing is an open hatch from heaven, spilling out rose petals and rainbows into our lives. In truth, some of my biggest blessings have come through hardship. God uses hardship as blessing. As

My Will be Done

Lora Story's song says, "What if blessings come through raindrops, what if healing comes through tears..." These things are blessings and mercy in disguise. God blesses us with distaste.

As the truth of God's word come to our lives, our taste buds change. When it comes to strongholds, what if our prayer sounded something like: "Lord, each time I flirt with an area in my life that you are calling me away from, let it taste bitter to me. Let sin become detestable in my eyes and let it no longer taste sweet and pleasing to me. Change my spiritual taste buds to crave the things of Your Spirit, Your will and Your way—not from a place of fear, but love...the love You show me daily. Let me acquire a taste for the pure and right things from you, Lord; let me become hungry for You; cause me to crave You."

King David's psalm speaks to this, *"O taste and see that the LORD is good: blessed is the man that trusteth in him."* Psalm 34:8 (KJV) I find it interesting that David included two of our senses in this verse; taste and vision. If we have good vision, we know that we instantly see whatever comes into our line of sight, whether we want it to or not. But to taste something is an act of the will, and trust. To set something to our taste buds takes courage at times. But nothing solidifies what we see like tasting it. And this is the way our spiritual senses work: we taste of God's goodness, *then* we see Him and His plan for our lives revealed before our eyes. And we taste of God's goodness when we allow ourselves to sink our teeth into the ways of His Word and His Spirit. Worshiping tastes wonderful when we allow ourselves to submit to the Spirit's leading, seeing that God is good as He visits us with His presence. The Word becomes a delicacy in our mouths as we read the promises of God and start seeing them become real in our lives. We have to taste of His goodness. And in turn, His goodness can become the very source of repentance in our lives, for His word says, *"Or despisest thou the riches of his goodness and forbearance and longsuffering;*

not knowing that the goodness of God leadeth thee to repentance?" Romans 2:4 (KJV)

The goodness of God comes in many forms. It can be as simple as discovering truth about ourselves. The spirit of truth causes the scales to fall from our eyes revealing God's better plan. Once we taste of His better way, we wonder why we ever lived any other. I remember a time while driving in my car and experiencing a moment like this. I had to pull over because the truth about my life suddenly hit me like a ton of bricks. I was simply out of the will of God. From the side of the road at a Sonic Drive Thru, I cried out to God and said, *"Lord, I just need to come back home."* I knew where home was for me. It was back in His presence, back in His Word and back to His way of living. Facing the sin of my self will became like "guava" for me. I had to be done with it. I'm thankful He used spiritual guava to lead me home.

And it is my prayer that He continues letting sin become like guava, so that I will be done with those things in my life that are displeasing, distasteful to Him.

Lord, let us be done with guava.

My Will be Done

DONE

4 DONE EXPECTING SMOOTH

I fly a lot and I enjoy it. The hustle and bustle of security check-in can be irritating, but overall, the experience is thrilling. I even like it when turbulence hits. Call me strange.

I was on my way to California for a business trip when I found myself sitting by a precious little Muslim lady in seat F3. I had the aisle seat and she was sandwiched between me and another man to her left. She was Middle Eastern and wore the typical Muslim hijab with Islamic dress. She kept to herself mostly but would look over at me every now and then with a sheepish grin. I returned the smile. I did not, however, strike up a conversation with her or anyone else on the plane. I usually keep to myself, do a lot of thinking and prepare for my business event.

We were about three hours into our flight when we hit turbulent weather. I had flown through turbulence before but this was unlike anything I had ever experienced. It was as if God grabbed our plane, shook it like a maraca side to side, up and down, and directed us, like a paper airplane, straight at a bull's eye on a cloudy wall. At one point, every passenger gasped for air in unison as the plane made a drastic drop in the sky. It felt like we cascaded down the first hill of "The Scream Machine" at Six Flags. As the plane shook side to side and dropped, the quiet Islamic lady next to me grabbed my arm. She looked at me with fear in her eyes, continued clutching me as tight as she could, and began praying in a very excited and rapid manner. I prayed too, but quietly. I am not sure what language she was praying to Allah, but it was loud and intense. I prayed silently to Jesus. And just like that, the plane returned to gliding peacefully through the sky. The Islamic lady and I looked at each other, with eyes as big as saucers, shocked at what had just happened, threw our heads back and both died laughing. I cupped my hand on top of hers as she clung to my arm and said, "It's all going to be ok. We're ok. No need to fear." Then I leaned back in

My Will be Done

my chair and whispered, "Because JESUS is in control." Looking back at the situation, I wish I had said that so that she heard it.

The rest of our flight was pretty smooth after that. And the laughter continued. The airline stewardess approached our seat asking if we wanted anything to drink. The Islamic lady said in her broken dialect, "Nestle and shoooogah?" The airline stewardess said, "You mean you want Nestle Coffee ma'am?" The Islamic lady nodded "yes" and the stewardess poured her some black coffee. I gently handed the steaming hot cup to her, and next heard her say, "No shoooogah?" Then she blurted out, "Shoooogah! Shoooogah!" The airline stewardess had already given her attention to the passengers across from us. She did not hear the lady say, "sugar."

My sky partner took matters into her own hands. She stood up, all of about four feet eleven inches of her, flung her Islamic garb out of her way, reached over me to the refreshment cart and grabbed a handful of "shoooogah." She sat down, looked at me and we both died laughing again. She stood back up, looked down at me, and placed her pointer finger over her mouth, as if to say, "don't say anything about what I'm going to do next!" And with that, she started grabbing salt, pepper, coffee creamer, little straws, and napkins. She grabbed everything but the sandwiches stuffed in the drawers below! She plopped back in her seat and I could not help but laugh again. This little lady surely entertained me all the way to California! We really did not talk much after that. We both fell asleep only to be awakened by the captain's announcement that we would soon be landing.

Reminiscing about the event reminds me that the voice of Jesus is much like the captain's on my plane ride. Just as the captain warned that we would be experiencing turbulent weather, Jesus also warns that the ride before us is not going to be smooth. We should not expect it. Parenting is not always a smooth ride. No matter how much we raise our children to be God fearing, life can toss them into a turbulent, faith shaking sky. Marriage is not always a walk in the park. There will be hurtful times when our differences will aim us toward a cloudy wall. And as we age, even our daily health can seem like a bumpy ride.

Finally, when it comes to being a Christian in today's culture, fasten your seat belt. The ride gets even bumpier as our faith and taking a stand for Christ is severely tested. We are under fire like never before. But even in all of these things, The Captain's voice can be heard as He says.

"I have told you these things, so that in me you may have peace. In this world you will have trouble. But take heart! I have overcome the world." John 16:33 (NIV)

I am thankful that in Him we can always find peace. He has overcome every turbulent wall that you and I will ever encounter.

And no, it may not always be smooth, but praise the Lord that we are never alone on the ride. Because "JESUS *is* in control."

My Will be Done

DONE

5 DONE BEING GOMER

Gomer. That was her name. Hosea. That was her husband's name. He was appointed and anointed by God to love her. What is so unusual about a husband loving a woman with a funny name like Gomer? Well, when a woman has the reputation as the town harlot and God tells a godly man—a prophet no less—to marry her, it is as unusual as a woman named "Gomer" to our ears. But Hosea loved God more than he loved himself and obeyed the extraordinary instruction. And he did not stop at marriage; he had three children with her and each of them represented the wrath of God toward Israel. This was not the typical picture of the model family; in fact, it appears—even by modern terms—to have been a recipe for disaster.

Before the wedding day, Hosea knew that Gomer was going to be unfaithful to him; the sanctity was sour from the start. And Gomer indeed proved to be unfaithful…numerous times. But God wanted him to love her regardless. And why would God make such an unusual request? The Father wanted to show His beloved and chosen people the extent in which He, Himself, pursued His own bride, despite Israel's continued and repeated betrayals to Him.

Like Gomer, we have each followed our own desires, pursuits of everything but God. We have crawled into the arms of "lovers" such as greed, impurity, covetousness, jealousy, self-indulgence—the list goes on. We have not affair-proofed our relationships with Jesus.

I am done being Gomer.

Something happens in the heart of a believer when, after years of wandering, he stops and says, "Wait a minute. Something has to give. I feel empty." Our unfaithfulness to God becomes as clear to us as a message in magic ink appearing on a blank, white, sheet of paper. And God chases our adulterous,

My Will be Done

idol-worshipping hearts with a fierce love until we embrace covenant with Him. That is how much He loves us. And the methods He uses to pursue each of us are unique to us, and surprising. Notice what God does to Baal-worshipping Gomer found in the following passages of Hosea Chapter 2:14-16 (NIV):

> *Therefore, I am going to allure her;*
> *I will lead her into the wilderness*
> *and speak tenderly to her.*
>
> *There I will give her back her vineyards,*
> *and will make the Valley of Achor[a] a door of hope.*
> *There she will respond[b] as in the days of her youth,*
> *as in the day she came up out of Egypt.*
>
> *"In that day," declares the Lord,*
> *"you will call me 'my husband';*
> *you will no longer call me 'my master.'"*

As I read this passage and heard a message preached from it recently, I wept...hard. To think of God Himself pursuing me, calling me to Him is enough to melt my jaded heart. And in a week where the words of others have been less than gentle, I was overcome by the gentleness of God's Word in my heart. He speaks tenderly.

As women, we crave tenderness. And God's vocabulary is sprinkled with gentleness and tenderness. It satisfies our cravings, if we stop long enough to listen to it. And where does God choose to speak the tender things? He chooses *our* wilderness, our dry, parched places. And there, God draws us to speak softly to us.

As I read this chapter from Hosea, I had to stop and back track a bit. When looking at the verses before the "alluring, speaking tenderly passage," I became aware of what I call the "pre-alluring" verses (9-13) that say:

Therefore, I will take away my grain when it ripens, and my new wine when it is ready." I will take back my wool and my linen, intended to cover her naked body.

So now I will expose her lewdness before the eyes of her lovers...

I will stop all her celebrations...

I will ruin her vines and her fig trees...

I will punish her for the days she burned incense to the Baals; she decked herself with rings and jewelry, and went after her lovers, but me she forgot.

These are very strong words and actions by God when dealing with Gomer. But it is exactly what God used to allure her as well. Her trouble became the place of her allurement. Her loss became the place for tender moments. Her place of ruin became the place of redemption. Gomer's heartache allured her to God. And at times, it is the very tool God uses to allure us. When we are lonely, God is alluring. When we have lost financial stability, God woos. In the middle of our idol worshiping and spiritually adulterous ways toward God, He leads us by His love and mercy to our personal wilderness. And there, He speaks. Our wilderness places become a sanctuary and holy ground, for it is where we become one with God; married, if you will. And just like Gomer, it is in the hard places that we come to know God intimately as husband rather than taskmaster.

My Will be Done

In your place of divorce, God becomes your husband. In the place of financial ruin, He is no longer a slave master, but provider and friend. In the places of death and loss, He speaks tenderly. And in the very place that you turned your back on God, your Valley of Achor becomes your door of hope.

God took many things from Gomer, but God never takes without giving something better in return. It is called restoration. God restored everything back to Gomer and will restore what has been taken from us, too. It may look different than before, but God promises to restore the years the locusts have eaten. Joel 2:25

I was discussing this "door of hope" and its meaning within the context of Hosea's story with my editor and he said to me: "Jesus *is* the door. And hasn't He already provided the way? He says, *"I am the way, the truth and the life; no man cometh unto the Father, but by me."* John 14:6 (KJV). And whether they understand it or not, this door—Jesus—will be the salvation of Israel in a very great mystery.

What a beautiful truth that our Valley of Achor becomes a door of hope. And Jesus is the door. When we wander, He is The Door. When we sin, He is the door of hope and of restoration. When we are Gomer, He is the door to newfound purity and covenant relationship with the Father.

And His restoration for us is the same as Gomer's:
I will plant her for myself in the land;
I will show my love to the one I called 'Not my loved one.
I will say to those called 'Not my people,' 'You are my people'; and they will say, 'You are my God.'"

As women, nothing feels safer than the words, "You are mine." It is a comfort to know that we are so valued we will not be shared with anyone else. That is what God is saying in this moment. So, today, if you find yourself in a personal Valley of Achor, the place where you turned your back on God, stop and listen. He says that we are His. We are safe. We are loved.   Let us flee false lovers…

And head for The Door.

My Will be Done

Be done believing that your best days
are behind you.
Your best days are ahead of you.

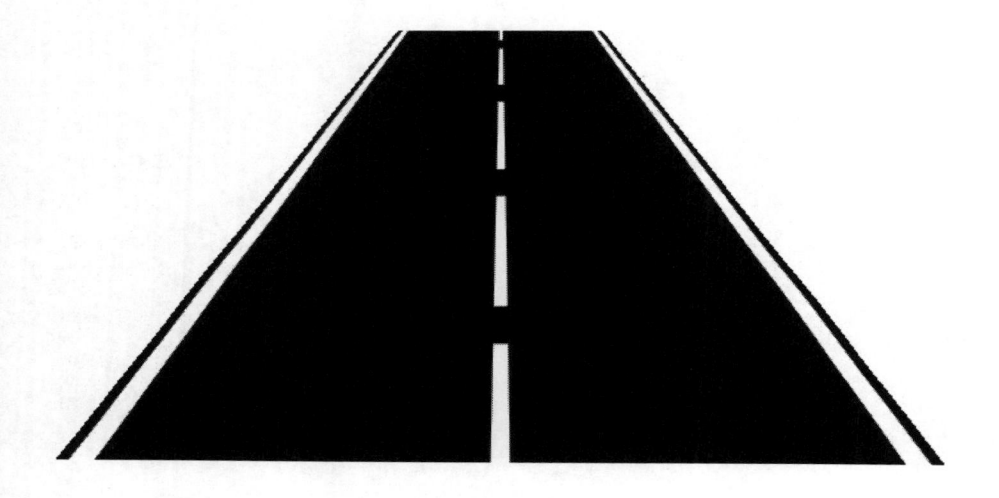

Haggai 2:9 *"The glory of this present house will be greater than the glory of the former house," says the LORD Almighty. "And in this place I will grant peace," declares the LORD Almighty."* NIV

6 DONE WITH NORMAL

Recently, I watched the movie, "Foot Loose," for the second time. I love the scene where Kevin Bacon stood before the complainers at the town hall meeting and read the verse to them from Psalm 149 that talks about David dancing before the Lord. The town was not happy about the idea of Kevin's gyrations corrupting their conservative Christian community. Dancing was not acceptable among "church people."

King David offended a few religious people, too. He laid aside his royal clothing to dance praise before the Ark of the Covenant, who enthroned God Almighty between the ark cherubim—in other words, he was dancing before the God of Israel. And he did so in a linen ephod, which is what *priests* wore. He removed his kingly threads to dance with a reverent heart before the Lord, and dance he did! Commentaries say he spun around in circles before the Lord. Others say he jumped and skipped as a lamb. By many, including Michal—daughter of Saul, David's predecessor—David was despised for his holy display. Later, as David returned to bless his household, Michal came out to greet him, saying, *"How the King of Israel has distinguished himself today, going around half-naked in full view of the slave girls of his servants as any vulgar fellow would!"* 2 Sam. 6:20 (NIV) Why could David not remain in his stoic role (as defined by others) and be reverent, eyes closed, hands clasped in his kingly robes? Be dignified, David!

It is paradoxical what we view as "normal" in our worship. Presently, I attend a church that is more free style in worship; dancing before the Lord, waving flags, or raising hands in worship are not uncommon. We distinguish between contemporary and traditional worship. When I was in college (not too terribly long ago!), I attended a church that was more traditional and that was just fine for me too. I appreciate all styles of worship.

I recently attended a church in Arkansas to be part of worship there. It was neither contemporary nor traditional; I would describe it as "simply authentic."

As I prepared by song list and thoughts, Saturday evening, I prayed over my list of songs and asked the Lord to help me decide what I should sing. I felt Him leading me to sing many songs I had not sung in a while even though my preference was to sing some of my newly recorded material. Despite wanting to assert my own desire, I decided to go with His leading. Before I entered worship with the flock the next morning, I was asked to join the church for breakfast in the fellowship hall. One by one, church members started joining my table and from the conversations that ensued—and my observations as an educator—I surmised that some of them were special needs adults. Later, I found out that the pastor had a real heart for special needs people and the church had a wonderful ministry to them in the local community. I could tell that they felt loved and accepted in this church and the church made a special effort to recognize their gifts and talents. It was wonderful! After hearing about this outreach, I remembered the importance of modifying lesson plans to reach such people. I pondered whether what I had prepared to say and sing was appropriate for the entire congregation. I quickly made some minor adjustments. By the time I completed my sound check, the church was filled with a little over three hundred special needs people and their families, waiting expectantly for worship to begin.

I was very intimidated and quite nervous as I wondered how I would handle myself, and whether I would be accepted. As so often is the case, I had slipped into making it about *me*. But I decided to follow the pastor's lead as he welcomed everyone to the service. I admired his finesse as he spoke to this beautiful audience with great tenderness and compassion. He was very elementary and loving in his approach. I decided to relax and trust the Lord to guide me.

Before the pastor introduced me, I was reminded of the evening before during my preparations. The songs God had led me to deliver a "simpler" message.

Waiting to be introduced, I felt the Lord was saying to me, "Thanks for trusting me. Simple is best." And so I stepped onto the stage and began worship.

I have never seen people more engrossed into the simple lyrics. In all of my years of ministry, this congregation was more in tuned than any ever has been. They understood the meaning of each lyric. And they worshiped. I sang "I Love You," written by my friend and Dove Award Winning Writer, Phil Cross. And as I sang about *my* love for Jesus, I noticed people starting to stand all over the congregation, expressing *their* love for Jesus. It was as if each person, and the body as a whole, had been carried away into their own world. No one was the least bit concerned about appearance. They worshiped with eyes closed, hands raised and faces lifted to Heaven; many sang along with me from their hearts. Others simply basked in the presence of the Lord. Some stepped out of their pews and moved to chosen spots of worship in the sanctuary--it was just them and the Lord. Others came and knelt at the altar with their families. And I thought to myself while singing that if strangers had entered the room just then, they would never have known the difference between me, and any special needs person in the room. Our worship was one. "Not normal," by today's standards, did not exist there in the presence of the Lord.

Worship transcended intellectual differences. There was no distinction between pastor, performer and congregation. We all were one. We were all draped in the "spiritual clothing" humility and servant hood. Their love for Jesus was authentic and

My Will be Done

unashamedly free. To be certain, there was no dancing or banner-waving, but God was worshiped in the purity of spirit; and it was definitely "Davidic." Their spiritual ephods were their pure hearts. And for me, the entire hour of worship with them was like a beautiful dance before the Lord.

As I gazed over the audience from where I stood, I could not help but think that their love for Jesus seemed greater than mine for Him. I considered the simplicity of their faith, and Jesus's words, "my yoke is easy, and my burden is light." Greek? Hebrew? Theology? Doctrine? Exegesis? I am fairly certain they know little of these things. But they know Jesus, and His perfect provision.

Lord, help me to come simply and "abnormally" to you and before you.

Help me be done with "normal" worship.

7 DONE NOT APPRECIATING MY INFLUENCE

Women have powerful influence. From our presence on PTO boards to CEO's of businesses, our influence is undeniably strong. But I believe our greatest influence is in our homes.

As mothers, we are keenly aware of the influence we have in the lives of our daughters. We shop together, share make-up and hair tips. We even wear each other's shoes and clothing when our girls grow up a bit. We giggle at silly things, cry at chic flicks and share cartons of chocolate ice cream mixed with tears when we are sad. But how strong is our influence when it comes to our sons?

I think we may have been given a bad rap when it comes to women raising boys, especially when it comes to single moms. We hear a cloudy and stormy forecast that says boys, when raised by single mothers, are more likely to be involved in crime, end up in same sex relationships and lose their faith, leaving the church (if they were in church). Some of this is true in *some* cases, but I would like to encourage an alternate view. The sunny forecast calls for connection.

If you are a single mother, raising boys, bless your heart! It is not an easy job. I found myself alone as a single mom early in my son's life and, for the most part, raised him and my daughter by myself. I did have the help of my family and am thankful for my mother's encouragement as well as the support of my father and sister. It helps to have Godly influences. But I am still learning that as a single mother, we are stronger than we think. I thank God for leading me through the difficult, beautiful road of single parenting. I am still walking. And it is from my journey that I write this chapter. I want to make clear that I have in no way "arrived." I am still learning lessons about "raising

My Will be Done

boys." Our influence reaches even beyond the empty nest. I surmise, in fact, that our roles become even more influential when they leave us.

I noticed a difference in the relationship with my son when he turned twenty. If had to pinpoint the time and place, it would be the day he left our home to live on his own, the day after I turned fifty. I was not prepared emotionally or spiritually for either, nor was I prepared for what happened next.

I had prepared for my daughter to go off to college. For months, we had planned decorations and new bedding for her dorm. We shopped for shower caddies, stringed lights to hang above her bed and more. The very day my daughter moved into her dorm, however, my son walked into our house and proudly announced, "Hey mom! My friends and I have found an apartment and we're moving in today. I'm here to get my stuff. I'm so excited!" And with that statement, I watched my son march up the stairs to his room, gather a few favorite books and things, kiss me goodbye, shut the door and drive off into the world of manhood and independent living. As the door closed behind him; silence and loneliness became my new tenants.

I came home from work the next day after both were gone and ate dinner alone. Missing was a greeting, laughter at the dinner table and even arguments about being late for school. My house was empty for the first time in years and the silence was deafening. I was alone and it did not feel good.

My son lived closer to home, while my daughter lived away at college. Ok, so she went only thirty minutes up the road, but she may have well moved to Oxford, England. With her involvement in music, she has not been able to be home much so I had extra time to spend with my son during his visits home, and we have become closer. We make a special effort to eat out each week, as well as Sunday nights; we can be found hanging out together at the house and sharing our favorite music with each other.

But I want to back up a few years, before moving on. When I carried my son during pregnancy, I was an elementary music teacher and had been for most of my children's lives. As a result, they were exposed to classical music, banging xylophones and recorders "in vitro."

During my son's pregnancy, I placed headphones on my stomach playing classical music: Mozart, Beethoven, Chopin and more. His Dad was a rocker. So while he got surround sound of the great classics from me, he may have also grown in the womb with Pink Floyd, Rick Springfield, Metallica and other bands. Some of you may be questioning our musical selections. I do appreciate all genres of music (maybe not *Metallica*) and I find it interesting now that my son's choice of music is Rock Opera!

On Sundays, he shares his rock-opera YouTube videos and I share a few gospel ones like Ethel Waters singing, "His Eye Is On the Sparrow" at Billy Graham Crusades. He and I both love choral music. His interest in it was sparked from gaming videos he played while growing up. (And that may be the only positive thing I can say about gaming videos: they play classical music and rock-opera.)

Sunday nights have been a wonderful time for the both of us to unwind and talk. Like most mothers, I enjoy scratching or rubbing my son's back. Listening to music gives me the opportunity. My son has long, beautiful dark hair, so like any good Mom, I like to rub his back and sometimes he lets me put a brush to his hair. I've learned to brush it rather than complain about it; those of you with long haired sons may know what I'm talking about. Anyway, listening to music like this with my son is a connection moment. But it does more than simply "connect" us and here is why: David played music for Saul. In 1 Samuel 16:23 it says, *"Whenever the spirit from God came on Saul,*

My Will be Done

David would take up his lyre and play. Then relief would come to Saul; he would feel better, and the evil spirit would leave him." (NIV)

That is the demonstrated power of God through music. There is likely a lot going on in my son's world I do not know about, nor probably want to know. But sharing Christian music is important to me because of the above verse. And it is healing for me as well. I choose hymns and sacred music when I get to choose because there is power in the Word—spoken, sung, or played. I use this time to pray silent prayers over his life while we relax and enjoy the moments together. He may never know or hear the words I pray over him, but God hears. And in the same way God used David's harp to drive evil spirits from Saul, I know God hears my mother's heart and moves in those moments. Moms? We have a powerful influence with our touch. Enter into that power.

To the extent you can, find a connection moment and spend time together. Talk. But mostly, I encourage you to listen.

The "setting" will be different for us all. For me, the right circumstance is listening to or playing music; even a drive in the car to Starbucks creates wonderful conversational moments together. These connections allow us to share truth in love, admonish with a caring spirit and simply show them Christ. *"Words fitly spoken are like apples of gold in a setting of silver."* Proverbs 25:11 (ESV) The right word, in the right time and place bears much fruit. Choose wisely.

Is my son perfect? No. We were all once fallen creatures, seeking redemption; once saved our true journey begins. We fall, but by God's grace, we get back up. Can we not simply be fallen and rally together?

I encourage you to consider your own influence, Mom. It is not the same influence that they will find with their fathers. Dad's role is extremely important and necessary; ours is different and should be. It was created to be that way. I often wonder if fathers realize how strong the love of a son is for his mother in healthy circumstances. And when mom is hurt, our boys hurt too. God is our healer. And even when divorce tears apart families—something God hates—He still waits there, stands there, pursuing, healing. God come quickly!

Jesus, the Great Physician, loved his mother. Above everyone else standing at his crucifixion, Jesus showed concern for his mother.

> *"When Jesus therefore saw his mother, and the disciple standing by, whom he loved, he saith unto his mother, "Woman, behold thy son!" Then saith he to the disciple, "Behold thy mother!" And from that hour that disciple took her unto his own home." John 19:26-27* (KJV)

These instructions from the Lord show His love and concern for His mother even when He was dying; He knew that a sword pierced her soul in that moment, as Simeon had prophesied thirty-three years before (*See* Luke 2:35).

I believe that the love a son has for his mother is simply another way God made man in His image. This unconditional love is from Him. Use your godly influence, fellow mothers. Find the time and let love grow. Your "connection moments" can be a powerful source of influence in his life.

My Will be Done

Be done thinking that your praise
does not ward off the attacks
of the Enemy.
Your praise is a weapon.

Psalm 149:6-9 *"Let the high praises of God be in their mouth,
and a two edged sword in their hand." (NASB)*

8 DONE BEING GOOD

Preacher's kids (or "PKs") live in a fish bowl. If you are one, then you know what I am talking about. Everything we do, almost every move we make as children, is not only in the public's view, but also in a not so silent, harsh and judgmental view. And our parents must be examples of perfect parents, "training up a child" and all that. So, we swim on, "being good." And because we do, we become very adept people pleasers. And when we don't please everyone looking through the glass, we develop a sense of false guilt and shame in our striving. Our lives become hyper-focused on measuring up to their crooked rulers, all for the sake of "being good." Well? It ought to say something that it took me until my fifties to be done with "being good."

This problem is not common to just PKs, however. As Christians, we are all under the world's microscope, for those close to us. But non-Christians and Christians alike, from a distance, keep their moral binoculars close by to scrutinize how we live, what we say, how we respond in crisis, even whom we choose to allow into our inner circles. Jesus and the tax collector come to mind.

But there is a fine line between raising our rebellious flags against the constant scrutiny and the biblical accountability to which we subject ourselves. Accountability—a term of Christian lexicon—has, or can have a positive impact in our lives because it encourages "right" living. And it comes from a place of love, not condemnation. God's Word commands us to *watch how we live, not being unwise* (Ephesians 5:15). It also says to be sure that we not cause others to stumble by our actions. (Romans 14:13-33) Again, the spirit of these mandates is not self or other-condemnation, but love of others over self. And it is our *motive* for obedience that is key. And too many times, fear of what others

My Will be Done

think *becomes* our motive. Does fear come from the Father? No. The result is that we walk in a people-pleasing funk, forgetting that we have been set free to live life fully.

If any biblical person had correct motives for living, it was Joseph, youngest son of Jacob. Joseph, if you recall, was hated by his brothers and sold into slavery. After having been rescued, he rose to a place of prominence and then was falsely accused of infidelity with his master's wife, Potiphar.

Potiphar was the palace guard's captain. Along Joseph's journey, he was sold to Potiphar as a household slave and while there, became an object of affection to Potiphar's wife. Scripture says that Joseph was "well-built and handsome." She set her mind on seducing him and day after day, asked him to come to bed with her. After finally escaping her clutches one day, the jilted woman lied to her household and to Potiphar about Joseph, accusing him of attempted rape.

How many men, today, or even then, would have been strong enough to turn her down, especially day after day? Lust in whatever form can come through the eyes, and it has long been stated that men are "turned on" by sight. Joseph was in the prime of his life, handsome and lonely. But he remained above reproach in his actions, avoiding her in the house, refusing her advances, and fleeing her desperate, final attempt to seduce him.

This biblical story reminds me of a situation involving my Dad that makes me smile. It ignites my admiration for him, too. He is a minister. He is extremely handsome and women notice! I have heard and seen numerous flirtations made about and to him. Ministers are not exempt from the approach of what I call "Jezebel spirits." I recall just such an encounter with my Dad on the lake one day.

My family was enjoying a day on the Tennessee River, when out of nowhere, a boat slowly passed in front of us. A beautiful, slender woman, wrapped in a bright colored beach towel, stood up on her boat and "flashed" us as she passed by. We were stunned at her boldness! She had no idea she just flashed a preacher. I think her towel would have stuck to her like Reynold's Wrap had she known. But there she was in all her glory, flashing her flirty smile along with her tanned body. What my Dad did next was amazing. His lips never broke a smile at the lady. He never once joked to us about her inappropriate display. My Dad looked at this woman straight on as she passed our boat and simply shook his head, "no," which rippled all over her foolishness. Silence fell over us all for a moment. But I loved the shout of my Dad's integrity. And I especially loved the way his "no" was completely honoring to my mother who was sitting next to him, jaw in the bottom of the boat.

I wonder if Potiphar's wife felt the same cold shoulder from Joseph's "no" as the bathing beauty that day. Joseph's "no" cost him. Cast into prison, the story continues, stating, *"But while Joseph was there in prison, the LORD was with him; He showed him kindness and granted him favor..."* Genesis 39:20 (NIV). Had I been where Joseph was? I am certain I would have questioned God about my dire straits. After all, Joseph had been faithful to God. God entrusted to Joseph visions, status, favor and *this* was his reward? It is one thing to suffer when we have done wrong. But there is an entirely deeper level of suffering when we do so under false accusation. Joseph suffered enslavement, imprisonment, accusation, and loneliness. And does this not explode to smithereens the notion that if we were simply "good" people, God would bless us and save us from trouble? Joseph was a "good man," but he had troubles—many of them.

But that is one thing that is great about the God we serve. He knows how to entrust and use trouble to show the Enemy the strength of Christ within a person. Joseph was a man of integrity and was planted within the fish bowl of prisoners, guards, and eventually, his own family. Trouble worked for his good. From where did his strength come? At one simple but enormous level, from his love for his God—not to please men.

I wonder if Joseph, living today, would have at least been a friend to Potiphar's wife. After all, aren't we supposed to remain loving Christians and not burn bridges with others? Let's put his situation into present day. Would Joseph have remained her Facebook friend? Ouch! He was so serious about his love for Christ that he "avoided" her. He protected his heart and spirit. Most of all, he protected his relationship with God. His obedience to God kept the favor flowing! Obedience brings blessing.

And what of Potiphar's wife? Scripture only mentions her seductive, lying nature. She remains nameless. And Potiphar is mostly remembered only for the sin of his wife.

What does the mention of my name bring to the minds in my fish bowl world? How about yours? Proverbs 22:1 says, *"A good name is more desirable than great riches; to be esteemed is better than silver or gold."* (NIV, Emphasis added)

I read this verse to my students while on a field trip in New York City recently. I asked them what they thought it meant. One student said, "It means that our actions and character are more important than all of Donald Trump's money!" I agreed. And I also shutter to think how my past mistakes have been dishonoring to my name and His. If it were not for grace, I cannot tell you where I would be.

Oh, to have Joseph's love.

I want to be "good" like Joseph. But I must remember Jesus' words, even of Himself in this context: *"Why do you call me good?" Jesus answered. "No one is good—except God alone." Mark 10:18* (NIV) This alleviates my burden to be "good" according to this world's standards. No one is good except God alone. As hard as we try, good behavior will never get us to Heaven's gates. God did not redeem us to be a perfect people, but to be "set apart," "in but not of," holy. And because of the cross, we are now the righteousness of God in Christ. Old things have passed away and all things have become new. (2 Corinthians 5:7)

Because of His grace, we can give a confident "Joseph 'no'" to our struggles.

Yes, I am done with being good…despite our fish bowl worlds. But I will never be done striving to live a life of obedience and loving Jesus more.

My Will be Done

Be done believing that your past has flawed your future.
You are flawless by the cross of Christ!

Romans 8:12 *"There is therefore now no condemnation to them which are in Christ Jesus, who walk not unto the flesh, but after the Spirit."* (KJV)

9 DONE BEING HOLY SPIRT, JR.

Christian women like "the change challenge." Show us a soul mired in doubt, drifting away from the faith or a blatantly unbelieving heart and our eyes become glazed over with a vision of "what could be." It's a good quality, but when corrupted in mere mortals at times, even a good quality can sour. And that is not so good.

It is a laudable thing that we have hearts of compassion as women. We are nurturers by nature. We have grown up kissing our dolls when they cry and hugging our puppies when they yelp. We are huggers, lovers, and well…Holy Spirit Juniors, or so we think at times.

It was not until this past year that I realized how many times I have spent trying to play the Holy Spirit in someone else's life. I heard a message from my pastor directed at married couples. Midway through his sermon he said, "Ma'am, I know you want him to change. And that's ok. But your job is not to be Holy Spirit, Jr. in his life. Your job is to pray for him and to love him. God is the only person who can change a heart." The pastor then delivered a few words of exhortation to the men. In a moment of *"Pastor*, Jr.," I wanted him to say, "And make sure you play with her hair every night," but that never came. (If you're a woman reading this book, did you just shout "Amen!" to yourself? If men only knew…).

Back to the sermon and the emphasis on prayer. His words were particularly freeing to and for me because I fail to realize—despite the promise of Scripture—just how powerful prayer can be. But if we are honest with ourselves, so often our prayers follow the spirit of country music rather than the Father:

My Will be Done

*Sometimes we get angry, but
we must not condemn.
Let the good Lord do His
job and you just pray for
them.*

*I pray your brakes go out
running down a hill
I pray a flowerpot falls from
a window sill and knocks
you in the head, like I'd like
to
I pray your birthday comes
and nobody calls
I pray you're flying high
when your engine stalls
I pray all your dreams never
come true
Just know wherever you are
honey, I pray for you.*

  I love this clever, honest song by artist, Jaron. While this, unfortunately, is often the way I *feel like* praying when I've been hurt or provoked to anger, it is way off the mark from the pose my heart ought to take in difficult times.

  The Word instructs us to bless and not curse our enemies. It exhorts us to pray. And when we pray blessing over someone's life, it means that we are asking God to do what only He can do to bring that life into alignment with Him, His will. The goodness of God leads a man to repentance.

 "*Or do you despise the riches of His goodness, forbearance, and longsuffering, not knowing that the goodness of God leads you to repentance?*" Romans 2:4 (NKJV)

When we pray blessing over someone's life, however, in truth we are asking God to show up. With blessing comes truth. With truth comes conviction. And with conviction comes the Holy Spirit to change a life. It is up to the Holy Spirit to arrange the circumstances in a person's life that will divinely create a need for God in his or her heart. This vocation belongs only to the Holy Spirit; our job is to trust Him. Then? We breathe! Changing hearts is neither our burden, nor our vocation.

In this vein, a family member of mine comes to mind. With this beloved soul, I have shared the Word and discussed lifestyle choices. But the more I do, the worse things seem to get. As you read this, perhaps one of your family members comes to mind. For my part, I was trying to be Holy Spirit's co-laborer. But after striving for too many years, the Spirit reminded me that my job is to love and pray. Period.

Has the Spirit's work in me correlated with any change in my loved one? Sadly, no. From regular church-goer to never attending; from struggling with the Body of Christ to exploration of other religions. My heart is seldom encouraged by what I observe.

Just a few weeks ago, I was in church and praying for him. I prayed that the Lord would bring him "home." That very day, he came to visit. He proceeded to share that he was "looking for his own truth." I bantered with him for a while, resorting to my "go to" sermonettes. But the Holy Spirit came over me, urging me to, essentially, shut up; I don't like being told to shut up! So, I listened.

After going on about his exploration into other world views, I blurted out something that surprised even me: "Great! I'm glad you are searching to find truth. Because ultimately, you will know the truth and it will set you free." I continued, "It is important that your faith is not anyone else's faith. It has to be *yours*. And when it becomes your faith, you will never forsake it. So good! Search it all out."

After uttering the words, I stepped back wondering, "Where did those words come from?" I basically had just told a loved one to keep looking into the occult.

You know what that did for me? It helped me resign my role as Holy Spirit, Jr., giving it back to the One for whom it belongs; I gave up control. Some might disagree, but as women, it is particularly difficult to relinquish control. And if we find ourselves in "control mode," it comes from fear. And fear is not of God. Let it go.

My sweet, soul-searching family member finally looked at me with tears and said, "…But I feel so dirty. I just want to find my way back home. I know I need to be in church again and I will. I just need to do my own thing for a while."

I slowly walked over to where he was standing, reached out my arms, hugged him tightly and said, "You will. You will. You will find your way. I promise. Because I'm praying." I asked him if I could pray with him before he left. He agreed. What I did not do was slip back into being God's supervisor. I got out of the way. I just loved him, and prayed—a moment I will not soon forget.

My sincere family member said to me: "You know…in my search…I have found that other religions are very self-serving. That is the one thread they all have in common. They have selfish ambitions and motives. I am finding that Christianity is all about serving others. It is the most selfless of all religions and seems to focus on others." I took that opportunity to say that Jesus was a servant. Christianity *is* about serving others. That is why I, and many members of his family are in ministry. We want to help others. We want to share Jesus because we know that that is what humanity needs above all else.

So, his search—though a bit scary for me—has led him to find truth. My job, and what God asks all of us to do, often? Wait on Him. Trust Him. Continue doing what we see the Father doing, just like Jesus did. Draw away from our harried lives and listen to Him.

My beloved family member continues his journey and searching. I pray and wait.

With loved ones especially, there is usually familial history. We have seen their junk—they have seen ours. The mission field here is most difficult. But God has resources we do not have. At times, I pray for angels, planters, waterers whom God can anoint to bring a message that my loved one just would never receive from me. Less of me, more of Him. Be patient.

My Will be Done

Be done with your timing. His timing is perfect.

Ecclesiastes 3: 11 *"He has made everything beautiful in its time. He has also set eternity in the human heart; yet no one can fathom what God has done from beginning to end."* NIV

10 DONE WITH STOOPING

Growing up in the south, the "language" must be learned over time. For example, "bless her heart," when spoken by a true Southern Belle (with batting eyelashes), could be interpreted as a sympathy by the uninformed, but is more often a sarcasm implying that "she doesn't have a clue, honey." And it is not uncommon for our visiting aunties to reach for us with a huge hug saying, "Gimme some shuggah!" as licked thumbs wipe smudges from faces. And one of my favorites is when a southern mother yells at her kids from across the grocery store, "git back over here! Ya'll quitit!" And "stoop," as in "Done Stooping," when referring to the body means to "duck or bend; to lean one's head or body forward." As used here, in a faith context, well, let us hear from my sweet friend, Mrs. Rose.

Mrs. Rose is the secretary where I work. Each day Rose and I discuss what the Lord is saying to each of us. I will see her and say, "Hey, Rose! What is the word of the Lord today?" I am constantly amazed that the Lord speaks the same word to Mrs. Rose and me. It is as though He whispers a scripture in her ear in the morning, and the same word finds its way to my house before school. In fact, I cannot think of a day yet that Rose and I were not on the same page when it came to "The Word of the Lord" for the day. Recently, Rose said, "The word of the Lord today is, 'Jesus, I trust You'" And with that statement, I hugged her and said, "Friend, that is *exactly* what God said to me this morning! We are still on track."

That same morning while I was brushing my teeth I thought about what it means to truly trust God during the tough times in life. I recalled my Dad's words recently: "Our faith is not in our heads; it is in our actions and the words that flow from the wellspring He creates in our hearts. He went on to explain that this is why Jesus said, *"Truly I tell you, if anyone says to this*

My Will be Done

mountain, 'Go, throw yourself into the sea,' and does not doubt in their heart but believes that what they say will happen, it will be done for them." Mark 11:23 (NIV)

I thought about my faith and the importance of the words, *"…if anyone says to this mountain."* If I *say* it, I must say it aloud. So, considering a few obstacles that are in my life at the moment, I stood in my bathroom and audibly said, "Lord, I trust You." And driving to my job that morning, whenever fear or uncertainty crept over me, I would say, "Lord, I trust you." Each time I did this, I sensed that fear dissipated and faith became my companion.

At lunch that day with Rose, we discussed our faith and how the words, "Jesus, I trust You" would continue to be the Word of the Lord each day in our lives and occupations. Regardless of what happens, "Jesus, I trust You." Whatever problems arise, "Jesus, I trust You." In every situation, "Jesus, I trust You."

As we finished lunch, Rose reminded me of something I too often forget. "Sheri, the purpose of the trial is to test our faith. God wants to see if we will trust Him, no matter what He allows—good, bad or ugly. And the testing may be the *only* reason for the trial. So trust Him even when you do not understand. Keep your faith up and don't let it "stoop."

Mrs. Rose simply meant "don't bend under the pressure or weight, nor succumb to doubt and fear, but rather, stand tall in your faith." Thus, "In regard to my faith…I want to do as Mrs. Rose encourages… and be done with stooping."

Keep your faith strong.

"Jesus, we trust You."

11 DONE WITH LA LA LAND

As little girls, many of us grew up mesmerized by the beautiful princesses in our bedtime story books. For me, it was Cinderella. I admired her so much that I wore her beautiful face mask with pink lips and large blue eyes for a Halloween costume. I graced the neighborhood in my gorgeous imitation ballroom gown made of icy blue satin and white lace. I greeted passing trick-or-treaters with my princess white gloves, never once wincing at the frigid October night air; Cinderella would never downplay her gown with a bulky winter coat. Nor did I keep my feet warm with ordinary cotton socks; because a princess must display her pink pedicure for all of the kingdom to see, especially in her sparkly Wal-Mart slip-on "glass slippers."

I loved Cinderella and envied every part of her magical world. From the ball, to the gown, to the prince who loved her; I wanted her world. But the entire notion of Cinderella and her life messed me up. Unrealistic expectations in this little girl's mind—bolstered by so many other images from my childhood—wall-papered my La-La Land castle. And even today, I occasionally catch myself peeing off shreds of perfectionism, unrealistic expectations, and mistruths from the hallways of my mind and memory. So, I have decided to re-model by visiting each room in the castle of my heart, to replace pictures, comfy lounging spots, and even—when necessary—completely tearing out entire walls. Things are getting raw and real in my kingdom.

I decided to have a "get real moment" with a few of my music classes in the all-girl, inner-city school where I teach. I shared with them the story of Cinderella and posed this to them: "What unrealistic notions has the story of Cinderella carried into our lives? How has her story tainted our world view?" Here is what they offered:

My Will be Done

1. Step mothers and step siblings are mean.
2. We believe glass slippers are comfortable.
3. Prince Charming is the perfect man and we are willing to wait forever for him.
4. The clock striking midnight means that time is running out for us too; aging stresses us out.
5. No one else in the world wears my shoe size.
6. Housework is shameful and degrading.
7. Perfect love can be found without actually knowing the person.
8. God is a lot like a fairy godmother.
9. The charming Prince did not know Cinderella very well: he did not know her shoe size (not a complete shocker for many men perhaps).
10. He had no idea where she even lived, or anything about her family.

I love the wisdom of my teenaged girls. Their analysis caused me to ponder more than a few of my own misconceptions. Let us consider a few that struck me the most to see if we can take some encouragement as sisters in the Kingdom.

"We perceive God to be a lot like a fairy godmother." Wave the wand and blow some magical dust my way! At numerous times in my life, my honest expectation has been for God to do a "fix all" with a wave of His heavenly wand to repair in a day, what often took me years to wreck. He loves us after all. And it isn't that He is not capable of such miracles; He is. Through my writing you will see a heart for unsaved family members. I forget that families are the most difficult mission fields, but still I expect my "fairy godmother" to simply apply the quick fix to the lost family members for whom my heart breaks.

Or, when debt and the cost of just living overwhelms me, I want God to pay it all off by some miracle. I confess that I bought a lottery ticket recently when the jackpot grew to the largest ever—over a billion dollars. I had a shot just like everyone else, right? And surely my grounded faith would prevent me from changing were I to win! Just give me that heavenly "Bibbidy-Bobbidy-Boo." I did not win. And when I give serious thought to the implications of a winner, I am glad I did not.

But for me, it is not just the substance of my prayers; I want them wrapped up in the magic moment *before* midnight. Is God ever late? Consider that notion for a moment. If He cares for us, knows our hearts better than we do, has a divine plan through which His ultimate victory and glory will come, then who am I to *ever* get frustrated with Him? More likely than not, He has already answered. So much of the Old Testament and the Hebrew nation is a picture of us—our hearts. How many times did the Israelites wander away from the Father's specific ordinances and precepts? It took prophets like Isaiah to recall the truth to their minds: *"Before they call I will answer; while they are still speaking I will hear."* Is. 65:24 (NIV)

And on this side of the cross, how much more has He done already?

Now for the glass slippers. All of us have glass slippers. Yet, unlike Cinderella, who never stumbled in her shoes, we do stumble and even fall in ours. And although Cinderella did not choose her glass slippers, we *have* chosen our shoes. We walk in what looks beautiful and pleasing to our flesh, but ultimately ends up in disappointment and even ruin. Unfortunately, we became attracted to sin displayed like beautiful glass on turn table under the world's bright lights. And we have danced in those shoes far too long, only to find ourselves barely able to walk. But that's where God meets us, picks us up and carries us to healing. Oh for righteous shoes.

My Will be Done

Finally? Prince Charming. There he stands. Tall, dark, handsome–ready to meet our every need. If discouraged, Prince Charming better make sure that he waltzes us into encouragement, or he is no longer welcome on our dance floor. When we are sad, He knows what to do: a spin on the dance floor into laughter and bliss. And I have a tendency to want the display to be public, I confess. Just to dispel any notion that I do not hold the prince right where I want him, and him, me. With his perfect smile, confident demeanor, and godly aura, I walk arm in arm with him on to the dance floor of perfection. And so it goes. My belief that "this is the one" who can complete me, disregarding the little fear-filled voice constantly whispering "but what if he sees you for who you really are?" So, I hide behind the waltz, my dress...and my glass slippers.

And the clock strikes midnight.

So here we are at the end of La La Land. Exposed. My castle has been a bit unrealistic filled with expectations that no one can meet. I am done with walls here that keep me from being transparent before God and man. I am done dancing in shoes and on ballroom dance floors to songs of my own making. And I am done thinking that a wave of the wand is going to give my castle and myself a sudden makeover in one "Bibbidy Bobbidy Boo."

The Christian life is not a fairy tale. It is real, and raw. However—and I love "howevers"—sometimes God does allow fairy tale endings to our sad stories. Like Cinderella, He interrupts the mundane of our lives and waltzes us into "better than before." And I will gladly wear my dress of expectation for His will for those times and all times to follow His lead.

I can hear Him say, "May "I" have this dance?

12 DONE WITH INSECURITY'S VOICE

"Put away the crimson painted drama claws and get on with your life." That is from I Sheri 1:7. If I were an apostle, I would add that verse to the Bible. Tongue in cheek, of course, but we women are known for drama. And we label *ourselves* that way. In my view, the drama we create stems from insecurity, and the voice of insecurity is pervasive and can be all-consuming.

I'm done listening to that voice.

We are all different of course, but we suffer from insecurity universally. Varicose veins, big butts, thinning hair, age spots: the list is endless. The lying voice inside reminds us that we do not quite measure up, and becomes an intertwined vine in every part of our lives. If we are fortunate, it is self-contained, not impacting those we love. But, it almost always does.

The voice of truth? Or insecurity? Which will we choose?

Insecurity screams one command: "Compare!" We compare our jobs, our incomes, social status, looks, and clothes. We become exhausted just trying to keep up. Why? Cultural cues? Is it generational? Did we learn it from a controlling parent? An absent one? A critical parent? Ponder and pray for God to reveal you the source. Stop insecurity in its tracks.

Compare those messages with the voice of God. Ezekiel 43:2 describes God's voice as being like "the voice of many waters." I just returned from teaching at a music conference in Pasadena, California. While there, I was fortunate to visit Laguna Beach. Wow! The biggest waves I have ever seen crashing against the rocks; the sound was majestic, powerful and peaceful at once. And that is how God's voice is. For many of us, God's voice is necessary to drown out the subtle, scrutinizing voices of our pasts. I am thankful for His unrelenting voice.

My Will be Done

Every single day of your life, you can hear one of two voices. One wants to say, "You cannot overcome this; it will ever haunt you." The voice of God, however, says, *"I am the Lord your healer."* Exodus 15:26 (KJV) Listen to the "still small voice;" it is awesome, and overcomes all others, if we let it.

Insecurity says, "You are your past." God says, *"Therefore, if any man be in Christ, he is a new creature; old things are passed away, behold all things are become new."* 2 Corinthians 5:17 (KJV)

Looking into my past, I recall the voices of two boys on the second grade playground of Bess T. Shepherd School. My friend and I would swing every day and they would shout their insults and we returned them in kind. They never became angry; they thought it was fun! My friend and I were furious every day.

I knew exactly what to do. I told my grandmother—the queen of telling it like it is. Sure enough, the voice of my grandmother resonated through the kitchen that day, "You tell those boys that if they don't leave you alone, your grandmother is coming up to that school and setting them straight! They better leave my baby alone!" Don't you love it when your grandmother refers to you as "my baby?" She's ninety-five and I am still her baby!

Sure enough, the next day at recess, I was ready for battle. My friend and I jumped on the swings and I was armed with my grandmother's artillery. Our harassers showed up and I let them have it: "My grandmother said that if you don't leave us alone…!" The two boys looked at each other, laughed their foolish heads off and moved on. They never bothered us again.

I recall that story because to me it is illustrative of the way we ought to address our wavering lives: call on our Heavenly Father, by and through the Word, and in prayer. We shoot down the accuser with the artillery of God.

In the face of failure: "*I can do all things through Christ who strengthens me.*" Philippians 4:13 (NKJV)

When we feel unworthy of love, life and family: '*Fear not: for I have redeemed thee, I have called thee by name; thou art mine.*" Isaiah 43:1 (KJV)

And in the darkest moments of our lives when we fear the past, future and the very day in front of us, we know that "*The Lord is my shepherd....*" (Psalm 23). His Word is the voice of our security.

The only way to be secure in the Lord, however, is to *accept* Him as Lord. Have you done this? You can trade in your insecurity today by praying this prayer sincerely:

God, I need You.
I have listened to the voice of insecurity long
enough.
I am ready to hear Your voice over my life,
blocking out all voices.
I pray that You take my insecurity and give me
security found in You alone.
Thank You for the cleansing blood of Jesus and
the cross that is my only eternal security.
Thank you for a new life, a new way of living.
Lord, if anyone looks at me from this prayer
forward, let them see Jesus.
Clothe me in righteousness. Let You alone
become the drawing magnet of my life."

If you prayed that prayer, congratulations! Say hello to security in Him, and a life you never thought imaginable.

You are done with any other voice.

My Will be Done

Be done believing that your present age dictates your future opportunities and limitations.
God renews your youth.

52

39   64   **48**

26 **73**

...who satisfies your desires with good things so that your youth is renewed like eagle's." Psalm 103:5 NIV

13 DONE WITH THE EXPIRATION DATE

As an empty-nester, there is a standing joke around my house whenever my son or daughter pop in for a visit…and some nourishment. Not long after the fridge door opens I will invariably hear, "Hey Mom! The milk has expired!" All too often it is true. I suppose I need to get the milkman on a regular schedule.

In a similar way, I frequently open the door of Heaven and yell, "Hey God! Remember that prayer I prayed two years ago? Well, it has expired!" I tap my foot, look at my watch, and hastily expect Him to "bust a move" on my request.

I am done with expiration date prayers.

I get frustrated while my prayers sit in Heaven's waiting room. And I picture them like those overlooked, undelivered meals in the serving window of restaurants, getting stale. In the same way I get impatient with late meal service from time to time, I grow weary of waiting for what I want! The nerve of God. The virtue, patience, is not at the top of my list. But what I fail to realize all too often is that God—in His infinite wisdom and timing—is preparing my answers.

Who can say that within God's perfect will, we know better than Him what the best timing is for any outcome. Christ promises that what we ask of the Father in His name, God will surely grant. What He does not promise is that it will be served up according to our calendars. We must, at times, walk in obedience…and simply wait.

The waiting reminds me of a child learning to ride a bike. As parents, we start them off with training wheels to build confidence. Some kids impatiently want to "take 'em off" to show they are ready and sometimes they are. But the balance is what must be learned and no one can describe what that balance

My Will be Done

really feels like. Without balance, however, the successful solo ride just won't happen.

Right now in my life, I am single. There are times I want to yell, "Hey God! My clock is expiring!" But I am learning lessons while still single that will be vital for me to carry into another marriage, should God grant it. If you too are single, I would like to encourage you.

Throw away any notion that as a single woman, God cannot use you for his glory. You know better. Even though my earthly heart desires a mate, I see that what Paul says about devotion to the Lord is true. I believe I clearly hear His voice and see opportunities to respond to His call. I can honestly say that my first time around (in marriage), I took for granted my heavenly relationship. "God's always been there; he wants me married, so, it will all turn out just fine!" But it didn't. And now I have the time to see that my deepening relationship with God is necessary before I cleave to another. So, with my "training wheels on," God prepares me by enhancing my prayer life, becoming more knowledgeable in His word and stronger in my faith. And if that day finally comes when He lets me go to matrimony, I will be better equipped to be a spiritual help mate to that chosen person.

Ladies? Keep those training wheels on until God introduces you to someone who appreciates your spiritual strengths. Every man needs a spiritually strong woman, just as a woman needs a "pastor" in her home. I know, I know. He may like your stilettos and your little black dress, but when the road gets salty, your spouse needs and wants someone who will storm the gates of hell with him. Build your spiritual might while you wait.

I met my college choir director for lunch the other day at Cracker Barrel. He is in his eighties now and has had a profound impact on my life. When I arrived, he was alone, waiting at the table. I snuck up on him and gave him a big hug, then sat down beside him. The first thing he said to me was, "Sheri, a man will die early if he is lonely. Thank you for being one of the many people in my life, along with my wife and family, who keeps me from being lonely."

That blessed me big but hit me hard too. I realized that God has placed so many people in my life who keep me from being lonely, and in this way, He has been answering my prayers all along. The spoken word of a true friend and mentor opened my eyes once again to the amazing love of my Heavenly Father. With training wheels on, I continue to balance obedience and prayer, so that I can be assured that God goes before me.

For whom can you be thankful? How is God answering those "stale" prayers you have long since forgotten about? Or, has He already?

If you struggle in singleness, recall with me that God's good and perfect will knows no bounds. Remain true to your calling; learn balance and contentment and let Him go before you.

Training wheels.

No expiration date!

My Will be Done

Be done believing that men are intimidated by strong, successful, women. A man striving to honor God by sacrificing for his wife appreciates, honors and needs a strong life partner.

Proverbs 31:1 *"A wife of noble character who can find? She is worth far more than rubies. Her husband has full confidence in her and lacks nothing of value. She brings him good, not harm, all the days of her life."* NIV

14 DONE WITH ALZHEIMER'S FAITH

Inasmuch as a person can be diagnosed with Alzheimer's in this life, my Dad has been. Dubbed a "cruel disease"—stealing moments and memories from its victims and families—it has not yet suffocated my dad's pastoral wisdom and faith. We are hopeful that it never will. Many sufferers pass from this life still singing the great hymns of faith and quoting scripture to their final breath. My Dad's faith seems stronger than ever; he does not have what I call an "Alzheimer's faith."

By this, I do not make light of anyone's suffering with this excruciating illness; I see what it is doing to my Dad, and to the woman who has faithfully stood by him for over fifty years.

As a preacher's kid, I saw my Dad endure serious battles. He suffered the death of his mother and my younger sister in a short space of time. He has survived church splits, church people and seasons of abysmally meager church offerings. I have watched him handle drunks from the street strolling in for worship, who would raise a right hand with a hallelujah, while their left longed for the next fifth. I have seen him treat the mentally ill in ragged clothes and sideways toupees with the same respect as the town's most highly respected dermatologist. I never once heard him complain when cutting short a family vacation because a church member suddenly passed away.

I watched, too, as his faith remained unshaken when the same families for whom he sacrificed vacations abruptly became sheep-shifters and left his flock. He wished them well. His faith remained.

And still does.

I had dinner with him and my mom a few nights ago. His face dropped as he said, "Well, we have bad news."

I asked, "What is it, Daddy?"

He said, "The roof of the church needs replacing."

My Will be Done

We all sat in silence at the thought.

He shook his head in disbelief just thinking about the leaking roof and the financial mountain that was before him and his small congregation. Then he gazed straight into what I call "his heavenly zone" and announced, "But I believe. I believe. The Lord has never let us down yet. And He will come through."

And I looked at my mom for her reaction. Supportive of him as always, she nodded her head in agreement, as she whispered with her eyes closed, "I believe, too. I believe." Their faith is unwavering.

But I sat there looking at both of them and wondered where my faith goes at times of severe testing. And I thought about where I have seen it "go," which fits for me because I have seen my faith slip away and "go" straight into the abyss! I forget God's power and His faithfulness. I have forgotten His provision. I have failed to remember his promises and His blessings. I have had an Alzheimer's faith. But I am done with it.

Bring on an "Essential Oils faith"—an anointing oil faith. Rosemary oil is supposed to help memory. I want a Rosemary oil Faith.

While listening to Dad confessing his trust in God, I obeyed the Fifth commandment, while breaking the tenth! In that moment, I loved and honored my father, but I coveted and wanted to take every ounce of his faith, were it something I could grasp. If only I could wear and show off faith like a piece of jewelry. We do not think of faith as a tangible thing, but in fact, God's word says it is. *"In addition to having clothed yourselves with these things, having taken up the shield of faith, with which you will be able to put out all the flaming arrows of the evil one..."* Eph. 6:16 (ISV)

Faith is a shield and is intended to be carried. I watched the fiery darts of doubt and discouragement fly straight toward my mom and dad that night. But faith extinguished them on the spot. They chose to hold up their shield. I saw how hopelessness tried to ease its way to the vacant chair at the table, but faith was comfortably occupying that place, and there was no room for despair. Hopelessness winces at faith's shield. I want that shield.

After we finished dinner, my mom said to me, "Would you like to go by the church and see the Christmas decorations? We decorated the church so nicely this week."

I wanted to and did.

I followed them in my car thinking about how they took such pains to decorate Dad's church, which was in desperate need of repair. The rain began to pour as I drove thinking how the leaky roof was likely causing more damage. But I recalled my Dad's words: "I believe. I believe."

I arrived at the church and watched my mom anxiously unlock the side door. She could not wait to show me the beautiful decorations. Her touch always enhances the church's warmth at Christmas. I expected nothing different this year.

I followed her up the stairs and we entered the dark auditorium. Excited, she said, "Let me turn on the lights!"

I watched her hobble up the choir loft stairs to turn on the lights. Just one little click and the entire pulpit came alive with beautiful white lights that decorated trees, wreaths and other greens. It reminded me of being at the amusement park just down the road from my Dad's church as a girl, with all the rides illuminated. She was so proud of the decorations; they were beautiful to me. I remembered my dad. He was just standing beside me, unusually quiet, in the center of the church aisle. He too was admiring mom's decorative Christmas work, when I heard him whisper, "I believe, Lord. I believe."

Again, I wanted his faith.

It was in that moment, while watching my dad cling to and verbalize his faith through his Alzheimer's mind, that the Holy Spirit whispered to me, and the conviction followed: "Be done with a lack of faith." For me, this meant being done forgetting to recall God's blessings and provision in my life; being done with weak faith, complaining and whining. I knew right there, standing in the middle of Christmas, that I was done with my Alzheimer's faith.

The disgust with my personal faith was the first step of God doing a new work in me. Being sick of one's own sin is a good thing. Dissatisfaction is frequently the catalyst for change in our lives. It was as though I had been waiting for this moment—expecting it, really. Just as I had hoped to grasp my Dad's faith earlier that evening, I now desired to see my disgust in a human and tangible personification. It helps me to put "ugly" on such revelations. "Thank you, Mr. Disgust. You are my catalyst for change."

Dad and I meandered to the church steps as Mom finished tidying up a few decorations inside. We sat beside each other, my foot overlapping his. It was there on the steps that the Lord inspired me to write this book.

But it wasn't just standing in the church that changed me that day. What he said next crystallized the moment for me. Sitting there on those steps, my Dad and I revisited a conversation we had had earlier at dinner. He asked me about people in my life; people he had not seen in a while. He happened to ask about someone from my past whose name brings back painful memories. I tried to hide the hurt but my father knows me; my feigned smiles never fool him. I just shook my head as my eyes filled with tears. He spoke straight into my pain. "God drew the line, Sheri. Stop looking at the line. Do not question it nor stare at it. God has something beyond the hurt. Look past the line at what He has next for you because He wants you to see His purpose and plan. It will be better. Keep looking at the better plan. Do not meditate on things that crush your spirit. Let them go, for they only hurt you. Be kind to your own spirit and take care of your heart." Once again, the Light of my Dad's godly wisdom trumped the fog threatening to cloud his marvelous mind.

Has God drawn a line in your life to protect you, saying "No more?"

Maybe He has drawn a line when it comes to your need to control. "Let go." Or has He drawn a line to an unhealthy relationship in your life? "This is where the strife and contention end. I have something better. Wait for it in faith."

Perhaps like me, He has drawn a line with your Alzheimer's faith. "This is where I want you to start remembering my faithfulness and praise me in every situation in your life. Trust me as I lead." Stop looking at that line.

Look ahead.

Walk on.

And leave your Alzheimer's faith behind.

My Will be Done

D
 O
  N
   E

15 DONE NOT CALLING IT WHAT IT IS

I love to attend my nephew's high school football games. Everyone clangs their cowbells, yells, springs to their feet and cheers for every moment of glory on the field. Parents cheer their sons for the next "touch down!" The air is electric with anticipation and excitement. Often, however, the action is not so great for the guys in black and white stripes.

Poor guys! They get yelled at with every decision they make. Watch what happens when a flag is called on a play. An entire section of the stadium turns into one huge Godzilla, ready to attack. Sometimes the angry crowd obliterates the marching bands in the stands. "Hey Ref! Try opening your eyes and watch the game!," they shout. But the referees continue to call it as they see it and move on to the next play.

I have tried calling it as I see it, too, with situations in my life. I suspect you have know what I mean. The problem is, as Christians, we feel guilty for calling things "as they are." If we are afraid, we are told fear is not from God. At times, it can seem like being yelled at from the stands. "Hey you! Try opening your spiritual eyes and get some faith, why don't ya? You're not supposed to let fear play in the game!" So, we are told that fear has no place in the life a Christian and we live our lives with reality contradicting our emotions. So, like referees, we make the calls we see, sometimes in faith, sometimes in fear. The wavering can be exhausting.

We throw a penalty flag when fear tackles us for a loss. Next play? Faith breaks free for a touchdown! Listen to the applause when others see God use us.

"Touch down!"

Can we ever just be real?

My Will be Done

At times, our Christian walk is more like spiritual schizophrenia. We waiver between being a person of faith, or a person of fear.

Take King David, for example.

He knew about fear. And he knew about getting real with God and himself. When it came to being honest about the situation at hand, he called it like it was. He refereed his fear and his faith. As a boy standing face to belt buckle with Goliath, the Philistine giant he said, *"You come against me with sword and spear and javelin, but I come against you in the name of the LORD Almighty, the God of the armies of Israel, whom you have defied."* 1 Samuel 7:45 (NIV) David acknowledged the giant. He called out his opponent's plan of attack: *"You come against me."* At times, I think, we ignore what comes against us. David faced his adversary on the field that day. He named his enemy's weapons. Many of us, frankly, have difficulty acknowledging *one* problem, let alone four, like David. Notice that he did not "faith talk" his situation by ignoring or denying what he saw. He never said, "That sword does not exist. God does not want my faith to shrink by looking at your sword and spear. I'll just pray against it and it will go away." No. David looked at the giant and considered each enormous weapon of destruction. He called them what they were. We should do the same.

David was realistic about his enemy, His God, but mostly assured by the strength of his spiritual head. And so it was, after choosing five smooth stones, equipped with his trusty sling, that David knocked that giant off of his enormous feet with one skillfully flung stone right to the center of that mocker's forehead. When David proclaimed, *"But I come against you in the name of the LORD almighty"* his faith trumped his fear, and a giant fell lifeless to the ground.

We may look at David's heroism and assume he feared nothing. After all, he overcame a bear and fought a lion at one time with his bare hands. Don't you think that David was afraid during those moments? I cannot imagine the mental conversations David had when fighting those "giants." He obviously fought the giant of discouragement as well. Listen to what he says in Psalm 42:5:

5 "Why art thou cast down, O my soul? And why are thou disquieted within me? Hope in God; for I shall yet praise him, who is the health of my countenance, and my God." Ref (KJV)

David was frequently riddled with fear and a downcast heart. But he remained steadfast in his faith and faithful to God's commands to him. We each have room for a little Davidic faith in the face of life's challenges. Call those "Goliaths" what they are, but consider with me, more often, the "But…God…"

I went through a gut-wrenching divorce. It was something I never expected to experience. The voices of the church and my pastor-dad shouted into my head and heart. I did not, then, consider every weapon of divorce. As I look back, it pierced my peace of mind, cut me with depression.

"Got Fear?" Admission is the first step. You have acknowledged the sword and spear of your giant. You know what is coming against you. Trust grows. *"What time I am afraid, I will trust in Thee."* Psalm 56:3 (KJV) I love the word "am" in that verse. "What time I *am* afraid…" We will be afraid. But fear leads us to the altar of trust, and there? It becomes active. God uses all things together for our good: pain to instruct, illness for healing, isolation to know His presence.

Is there a fear overshadowing you? Name it. Call it what it is. "Be David" about it. Are you afraid that you will never see beyond the mountain of debt that stands in view of your future? Speak to the mountain in a Davidic fashion: "What time I am afraid of my debt, I *will* trust in God." Are you afraid of a recent doctor's diagnosis? Be Davidic with it, "What time I am afraid

My Will be Done

of cancer, I will trust in God." Maybe your marriage has crumbled. Call out the weapons, but consider your God.
Whatever the situation, referee your fear and faith.
Call it what it is.
Trust God.
With Him, we win.

16 DONE SLEEPING WITH THE ENEMY

Many of us have trouble sleeping at night. We can thank our friends, stress, worry and even poor eating habits for the nuisance. And many of us just pop a pill for the close cousins, anxiety and fear and we are good to go.

We look at Facebook and the news daily. We are "skeert" to death! (That is "southern" for the word "afraid" in case you are wondering).

Fear. What fear do you have in this very moment? We all have something. We fear everything from our past, the present, to worrying what the future holds. In other words, we make ourselves miserable with this four-letter word. Fear can be a consuming and debilitating monster. Fear cuddles up next to us every time we lay our head to rest. It whispers in the dark, telling us about the monsters hiding in the closets of our pasts. And it seems, at times, that just as we calm down from worrying, fear jerks the covers off all our hopes and dreams. Fear makes us miserable: it robs our peace, wrecks our nerves and seeks to assault our faith in the One who wants none of it for us!

In short, Fear is literally our enemy, because it is from THE Enemy.

And I'm done sleeping with him.

Many of us have been sleeping with fear for years. I spoke with the sweet grandmother of one of my inner city students traveling to New York City on scholarship with our singing group.

At school, the student told me, "Ms. Thrower, granny ain't gonna let me go. I'm tellin' ya. She says that's just too far for me to go!"

She was right! Her grandmother called me this morning and said, "Hello, this is so-n-so's grandmother. I'm callin' to tell

My Will be Done

ya that she ain't goin' on that trip! It's too dangerous and it's just too far. We ain't ready to let her loose like that yet."

After listening to the grandmother's fears of letting her child go on our trip, I tried to console her and let her know that I understood her concerns. She continued telling me that almost twenty years ago, a member of her family was walking home one day on a street in our school's neighborhood and "got snatched," as she described it. They never saw her again. She is paralyzed with fear because of that kidnapping. She is so afraid of the tragedy that took place that she is now afraid to let go of the reigns with her teenage granddaughter.

We can all identify with her story in some way in varying degrees. Thankfully, I have never experienced the horrible trauma of losing a child to kidnapping or death. But I have experienced other personal traumas, which resulted in emotional paralysis. Rape, sexual abuse and abandonment in all forms can leave us completely paralyzed, in all aspects of our lives: emotion, physical, mental, spiritual. There have been times in my own life when I figuratively flat-lined and was ready to welcome someone, anyone, to pull the white sheet over me, my life. Frequently, especially in the middle of those periods, the overwhelming sense of fear and numbness discomfortingly climb into bed with us every night. Then the darkness comes.

And when we wake up from what little sleep we have had the night before, we are traumatized by the same fear, the very same worries all over again; and we are exhausted, haunted simply driving to work, with fear whispering into our consciences, threatening at every turn. I am done sleeping with the enemy.

My Dad helped my son with a fear of darkness as a young boy. As with many young children, my son was afraid of the monsters in his closet and, particularly, the one hiding under his bed. Being the good preacher, my Dad pointed him to God's

Word and told him that sometimes we all fear things that do not exist at all, like monsters. At bedtime one night, my Dad opened my son's closet door and looked for the monsters. Nothing but clothes and toys. He then knelt down and checked under my son's bed. Vacant, except for some dust bunnies and missing socks. Then, my Dad pulled out one of his business cards and began scribbling like a doctor hurriedly writing a prescription. When he finished, he clicked his pen, put it back in his pocket, folded the card and put it on my son's dresser table. The card had this written on it: *"There they were in great fear where not fear had been; For God scattered the bones of him who encamped against you; You put them to shame, because God had rejected them."* Psalm 53:5 (KJV 2000)

I love that verse but had never seen it until my Dad wrote it on the card and placed it on my son's table. My son kept the card for a long time. Each time I cleaned his room, dusting his table, I picked it up and read it. It is so comforting and so true. *"They feared where no fear was."*

I have feared things that never materialized. In fact, don't the fears we spin on most often nearly never actually happen? *Oh the years that the locust consume.* (Joel 2:25) I feared a doctor's report that came out negative. I have feared the unknown at work, expecting the absolute worst outcome more times than I can remember. I was afraid every time my children drove away in the rain, only to receive a text saying they made it safely to their destinations. I have been afraid of new responsibilities, new opportunities, new people in my life and even love—both giving and receiving it. This is what happens when I allow fear to snuggle in close to me, ever desiring to convey its bedtime story into my mind.

I am done sleeping with fear.

In this day and time when fear knocks on our proverbial doors in the evening news, ever-looming bills, and the

My Will be Done

uncertainty of tomorrow, isn't it good to have His Word as our blanket and comfort? God tells us over and over in His word, "Do not fear." We should embrace these words in the night seasons.

Will we have trouble? Yes. Will we be traumatized by life's events? We may. But here is another verse of hope that may help in these situations—a well known passage from Psalm 23: "*...Yea, tho' I walk through the valley of the shadow of death, I will fear no evil, for thou art with me, thy rod and thy staff, they comfort me...*" KJV.

"Tho" is a key word: [even] "Tho" I walk; [even] Tho I hear the doctor's report; [even] Tho I may be abandoned, and [even] Tho I may experience every one or none of my fears at all, thy rod and thy staff--they comfort me. I will not fear. I love that the passage does not say, "I don't have to fear." It says, "I will not." It is a conscious act of the will that we make to not live in fear.

And I am making a conscious effort to not sleep with fear tonight.

I covet your joining me in saying, "I too am done." The passage does not say, "I do not have to fear." It says, "I will not fear." It is a conscious act of the will that we make to not live in fear.

And I am making a conscious effort to not sleep with fear tonight. I covet your joining me in saying, "I too am done."

17 DONE WITH HUNGER GAMES

If you have a teenager, you may well be familiar with The Hunger Games trilogy, which takes place in an unspecified future dystopian post-apocalyptic nation of Panem in North America. The country consists of a wealthy Capitol and twelve distinct districts ruled by the Capitol, which is lavishly rich with advanced technology. The twelve districts, however, exist in varying degrees of poverty. The trilogy's narrator and protagonist, Katniss Everdeen, lives in District 12, the poorest region of Panem, where people regularly die of starvation. As punishment for a past rebellion against the Capitol, known as "The Dark Days," one boy and one girl—ages 12-18—from each of the twelve districts (known as "tributes"), are selected by lottery to participate in the "Hunger Games." The games are then televised showing the participants being forced to fight one another until only one remains. The winning tribute and his or her home district is then rewarded with food, supplies, and riches.

I submit that, like the tributes' fight to the death, we as women "fight to the death" when striving to get our needs met. We want to be the best mothers, more attractive than our neighbors, to get respect in the workplace while battling our changing hormones, bodies and hair. We have been told by Madison Avenue, that we can have it all, and be it all, without apology to anyone. It becomes a game that we fight to win, but in the process—at times—we sacrifice our souls together with every last ounce of self-respect we've managed to salvage through it all. And we do it because we are hungry; and in our hunger pains, we look to everything but Jesus to fill the need.

Welcome to the Hunger Games.

They run rampant on our Facebook pages as our hunger tops the attention-seeking meter. And we are relentless in our manipulative schemes and plans to finally gain our prize—the

My Will be Done

knight. Our hunger shows from the way we dress, to the passive-aggressive remarks we post on our pages five times a day. We are hungry. I realize not all of you are on social media, but by the looks of it, most of us are...and we ran the millennials right off of it.

I call it being hypoglycemic in the spirit. I have hypoglycemia, which is low blood sugar. It is the opposite of diabetes as my sugar levels can drop lower than normal when I need something to eat. My body experiences shaking, blurred vision and dizziness. I have been known to faint on occasion.

Spiritually, we get the shakes when we have unmet needs. We are hungry. And our spiritual vision is blurred when we dig in and refuse to turn to God during our time of need. My blood sugar booster of choice is chocolate so I generally go there first. But in a similar way, we grab for the nearest "sweet" we can find to satisfy our hypoglycemic spirits.

We are hungry for love, a natural need given by God Himself. And when God does not fill the need according to our schedules or in the ways we think He should, we are inclined to reach for the "candy of sin" to meet it. But there are consequences for this proclivity. While we anticipate the candy bar to meet our longing, nothing else matters. Sin is like this. "God will forgive me," we say to ourselves. Commit the act. And then, *hopefully*, the crash. We find ourselves in the lowest levels of depression, anger and hurt. Then we grab for bitterness and resentment as our next source of nourishment. And the cycle continues. We are a hungry people. And worse, if we repeat this pattern too often, God says our consciences become seared to the guilt. We no longer care.

Jesus knew about hunger. And Satan knew just when to tempt Him. The enemy similarly comes to us in our weakest moment to destroy. So begin the Hunger Games. He sees a divorced mother, in need of love and attention. He sends someone who will play her heart and emotions, leaving her spiritually dead and lifeless. He sees someone alone and lonely and he sends someone out of fellowship with God to be her constant companion. And when we are tempted to reenter poisonous relationships from our past, we blame it on our hunger. The garbage can looks appetizing when we are in spiritual starvation mode. Give yourself a break. Hold a stop sign up for your heart and emotions to recognize it and say, "Enough."

I have had to practice this in my own life being single. There comes a point in our lives when we have to give our heart a rest. Divorce leaves us broken. Failed relationships leave us shaking in the spirit. We need nourishment in our hypoglycemic spirituality. As much as I know the Word of God and even teach it, if I do not "eat" His Word daily, I shake, my vision becomes blurred and I get desperate. We seek to avoid pain. It is a human response. How we do it makes all the difference. If we turn to the loneliest and void places to fill our hunger, we will actually remain hungry. It is a game.

At the time of this writing, I am just fifty-one and both of my children have moved out of my nest. It is a lonely time. And I have found myself hungry.

But I'm done with Hunger Games.

It is during the lonely and hungry times of life that I have to bury myself in Psalm 107:9, "*...for he satisfies the thirsty and fills the hungry with good things.*" (NIV)

When I am lonely, God is aware of my hunger. He is with me and will meet every hunger pain.

God wants us to give our hearts and souls a rest. He *wants* to fill us with good things. But we have to allow Him to stop our spiritual jitters, and wavering.

In Scripture, this longing seems more often acquainted with thirst than hunger. We can go weeks and weeks without food. But water? A handful of days and we are finished.

My Will be Done

I will close with the words of King David as he tells us what to do when we are hungry, or better, thirsty for Him. *"As the deer pants for streams of water, so my soul pants for you, my God."* Psalm 42:1 (NIV) When we pant or thirst, it is an indication of our need for God and nothing else. The Psalmist says, *"Taste and see that the LORD is good; blessed is the one who takes refuge in him."* Psalm 34:8 (NIV)

Taste of God's goodness before you reach for what your blurred eyes think will satisfy.

He will stop the shaking.

Be done with Hunger Games.

Sheri H. Thrower

Be done with the self-defeating attitude that you cannot press on in your weakness. You are stronger than you think.

Philippians 4:13 *"I can do all things through Christ who strengthens me."* BSB

My Will be Done

DONE

DONE

DONE

DONE

DONE
DONE

D O N E

18 DONE WITH THE PEN

As an author, I plan, think ahead, and am constantly fixated on "the story." I write what I know, imagine and have experienced in my past. But there comes a time when God takes the pen from my hand and writes a dramatically different middle, end and even beginning—at times—to what I have in mind or have already written. And as I look back at the first page of the chapter, or book, I often see a beautiful story of surprise, wonder and even reason all wrapped up in one complete and holy message that I could never have imagined. Consider Jesus's mom.

Her plan: Marry Joseph.
God's plan: Give birth to Emanuel then get married!
Welcome to "How God Works 101."
And Mary's response? "How can it be?"

I find myself uttering Mary's words often. The circumstances around me do not compute with the outcomes, the answers. Mary knew she was a virgin and naturally asked the question, "How can it be?" Every one of us who has experienced pregnancy would have done the same.

I find it interesting that when the Angel of God appeared to Mary to give her the blessed news, He did not come with a plan. He arrived with an announcement laced with an imperative: fear not. Imagine what a "plan" would have included.
Gabriel: "And on this calendar day, you are going to travel by donkey to Bethlehem and give birth to the Christ Child in a trough because all the rooms are filled up with travelers for the census! Good luck, Mary! I have to run another errand now, but do not be afraid!"

How would I have responded?

Yet God shows up. He asks us to do difficult things, self-sacrificial things. My will? Or His? Do I *really* believe in this?

My Will be Done

Will He not still carry out His plan without me? We can never know. He does not come to us to rob us of joy, but to give it. Abundantly. Fear not.

We may naturally and humanly imagine that Mary experienced fear and uncertainty as labor intensified and the barn stall was the only space available. Scripture says, *"But Mary treasured up all these things and pondered them in her heart."* Luke 2:19 (NIV) I must believe that if the holy vessel chosen as worthy for God's only Son had to "think about things," that God is ok with our pondering. He gives us time.

Mary's idea was an inn. God's idea was a stable. My idea for God's will is always a picture of comfort. My pen is ready to write a comfortable and reasonable story. But God's pen writes holiness.

Though often unrecognized today, God writes frankincense, gold and myrrh into our stories. Can you imagine a stable with all of those gifts? "Where shall we lay the gold for you, Mary?" asks one wise man. "And where would you like for us to lay the precious oils, Mary? May we set them here by the stall of hay, easily within your reach?" says another. Mary and Joseph looked a place where God first led them. It was place with only hay, straw, a feeding trough and almost certainly animal manure nearby. But once God's will had manifested, this "dirty" place was filled with great treasure. This is exactly what God does with our unclean places.

Allow God's pen to write your story of beauty and sacrifice. I am striving for this even as I continue writing down my stories.

I'm done with fear of His plan.

I'm ready for His beautiful.

And I will trust Him as He mysteriously combines my struggle into the ink of His perfect will, to write a story that glorifies Him. I'm done with "my" pen.

Sheri H. Thrower

HIS PEN TODAY... Every Day

19 DONE NOT RESTING

Someone posted a video on Facebook today of a family gathered around the piano singing the hymn classic, "I've Anchored My Soul in the Haven of Rest." I clicked "play" and I was cooked. I wept like a baby at the song's rich lyrics and the wonderful heartfelt harmonies of the singing family. The chorus:

>*I've anchored my soul in the haven of rest*
>*I'll sail the wide seas no more*
>*The tempest may sweep ore' the wide, stormy deep*
>*But in Jesus, I'm safe ever more.*

(Words and Lyrics by Henry Gilmour Born)

There is something irreplaceable about the older hymns that have withstood the test of time. Rich in theology and gut wrenching at once, they reach and speak to the deepest parts of our souls. And this song, on this day, spoke to me of the rest we find in anchoring ourselves in Jesus.

I have anchored myself in many things other than Jesus. We all do. We trust people, jobs, and savings accounts. And while these are all "good" or socially laudable things—meeting our needs—they do not provide *soulful* rest. Sometimes, we simply need to go to Jesus, and rest. And like the song says, "anchor yourself there."

The obstacles to rest are countless. Many cannot sleep at night, while others battle daily depression and are simply unable to escape their beds. This latter depressive sleep is simply a defense against conscious thought of our troubles: escaping pain. But true rest provides peace and true peace is found only in Christ.

What is making you need rest today? A suffocating marriage? Exasperating children? An overbearing and unjust supervisor? For me, a year just ended with many blessings but

My Will be Done

also deep loss. I am realizing some dreams but worn out from building them. I need rest.

So, let us anchor ourselves in His word, His music, Him. Plop yourself down in a comfortable place and posture and just "be." Remove the hats you wear: mom, wife, chief domestic engineer, friend, caretaker and just "be" before the Lord. Sit in His presence and let Him wash over you.

Rest.

Your mind needs rest. Your body needs rest. And those around you need you to rest as well. We spin our wheels at breakneck speed flying ninety to nothing through life, then present ourselves to our families out of breath and frazzled. Rest. Those important to you need you to rest. Mom, your baby needs you to rest. Try doing nothing, even if you are not a napper. "Don't just do something-stand there!" It is ok to take a nap when your baby does. Let the house go for a day and rejuvenate. Check out a mother's day out program in your area and enjoy peace and quiet. Whatever you do, set aside some time to rest.

Even Jesus took time to rest. His word in Luke 5:16 says, *"But Jesus often withdrew to lonely places and prayed."* He was the first true contemplative no doubt. He drew great strength being with His Father in these times. If Jesus Himself needed time to rest and pray, how much do you and I need the same? Notice that the scripture says, "often." Jesus withdrew to lonely places and *often.* How often do you recoup? I am not speaking here of sloth; that is another extreme, and an unhealthy one.

In this New Year, I am taking time to write. But reading works as well. If you are looking at next week, or month, then you may be exhausted before getting there. Rest. Recoup. Sit yourself down in front of a song that melts you like butter and let God refill you. Then set your anchor; re-anchor yourself in Him.

As I reflect on the year just past, I see loss, failure, hope, and success at once. Rest.

If you have been on the hamster wheel, be done with not resting.

My college choir director said to me recently, "One thing is for sure about stress. It'll kill ya." We talked about the importance of making room in our lives for less stress, or at least managing it better. The stressors will always be present. We cannot control how and when they come at us, but we can control how we face them. Rest is one powerful tool to accomplish it. When life is ripping your joy to shreds? It could be one person or a group of friends. Make room for peaceful people.

It is also vital to surround yourself with others who encourage and strengthen your faith. Who in your life encourages you the most? Who strengthens your faith? Be with those people and rest in their encouragement.

In the same way, let those "takers" fade away. There is nothing more draining than contemptuous people. In love, simply dismiss yourself. It will be alright.

Of late, I have redone my budget and started a new, lower paying part-time job. I have more time to rest. Peace is a precious commodity that money cannot buy. Satan has been lying to us Americans for years, lifetimes. We so easily fall prey to the lure of money and more money. In this moment I am enjoying a cup of Folger's and resting in the fact that my daughter is home from college. I hear her scuffling around upstairs. I will rest in how I love being her mom.

Rest.

My Will be Done

> Be done believing that you cannot be honest before God.
> You can just be you.

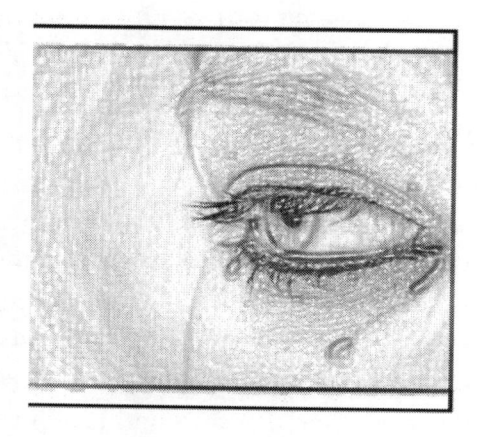

Matthew 11: 28 *"Come unto Me, all who are weary and heavy-laden, and I will give you rest."* BLB

20 DONE BEING HACKED

My Facebook was hacked this morning. If this has happened to you, then you are familiar with feeling violated--completely. Someone gained access to my personal information without my permission! The next thing I knew, I started receiving mounds of emails from friends telling me that they had received friend requests from me. Thankfully, someone texted me and said, "Change your password. Someone has hacked your Facebook account," which I did immediately; it helped me feel a bit safer, but not completely.

I am done being hacked, and not just in my Facebook account. I am done with the Enemy who breaks into the personal pages of my life in full invasion mode. It happens in my weak places, and more insidiously, in places I thought I had erected strongholds. Before I recognize it, frequently, I am a blubbering mess, crying and upset over my future, job, finances, relationships, and, yes, my looks and self-image. And following this emotional onslaught, I occasionally battle depression, anger, bitterness and on and on.

So, what defense do we have against these spiritual invasions? How can we be truly done with the Enemy hacking our lives, our peace? Like every good Sunday school answer, a safe bet is to look to Jesus. Prior to the beginning of His ministry, we find Jesus in the wilderness--alone.

Luke writes that Jesus is hungry from fasting and praying. Ever notice how when (if) you are truly hungry, that you can think of nearly nothing else but eating? Satan knows. He approaches Jesus with, *"If you are the Son of God, tell these stones to become bread."* In other words, make some food for yourself to satisfy your hunger. Jesus replies—knowing from where true and lasting satisfaction comes.

My Will be Done

"*It is written: Man shall not live by bread alone, but on every word that comes from the mouth of God.*" Matthew 4:4 (NIV)

Without oversimplifying, I assert that whenever Satan visits us in our weak moments and places, that we reply with "It is written…."

When we are fearful generally, it is written: "*God has not given us the spirit of fear; but of power, and of love, and of a sound mind.*" 2 Tim. 1:7 (KJV)

When we fear being alone, it is written: "*…lo, I am with you always, even unto the end of the Age. Amen.*" Matthew 28:20 (NIV)

When we are overwhelmed with sadness that lost souls in our family are dying without Christ, it is written: "*The Lord is not slow in keeping his promise, as some understand slowness. Instead he is patient with you, not wanting anyone to perish, but everyone to come to repentance.*" 2 Peter 3:9. (NIV)

And when we fear death itself, we can recall the words of King David who said, "*Yea, though I walk through the valley of the shadow of death, I will fear no evil: for thou art with me; thy rod and thy staff, they comfort me.*" Ps. 23 excerpt.

If Christ Himself knew the power of the Word over the Enemy, then why do we fall away and hesitate to invoke that same Power from on High? Sadly, and often, it is because we have not hidden the Word away; we have not digested it—the very Bread of Life. And how often do we find that our biggest condemner is our self. Self-flogging. We make it easy for Satan and become our own worst enemy. I often do not even realize I am doing it before I am in an emotional crisis. What remedy, what salve, what balm do we have? The spoken word—His Word.

Be done with hacking. Learn the Word. Speak it

I am done believing that God may not restore it *all*.
He restores the years, the days, the hours, the minutes…the moments.

Joel 2:25 *"And I will restore to you the years that the swarming locust has eaten, the crawling locust, and the consuming locust, and the cutting locust, my great army which I sent among you."* KJV 2000

My Will be Done

DONE

21 DONE WITH ENVY

I asked "Siri" the definition of "envy." The reply?, "Envy means a feeling of discontented or resentful longing, aroused by someone else's possessions, qualities, or luck." Have you ever been envious of another person or their things according to this definition? I have. Though there is grace, it is a clear violation of God's law. For myself? I have decided to be done with it.

Some people may be envious of another person's nice, new car. This one is not a biggie for me, nor most of my women friends. I suspect that cars are mostly a "guy thing." I am very happy with my Nissan Versa, thank you very much; it gets 42 miles to a gallon of gasoline on the highway and costs me only sixteen bucks to fill up these days. Nope! Not an area of struggle for me.

Still others I know strive for the lavish home with a pool and nicely landscaped grounds. They can have them. Dr. James Dobson, founder of *Focus on the Family*, shared—years ago—that we do not really own things like houses; they own us. I have neither the time nor the interest to maintain a pool or clean an enormous house (nor the means to pay someone to do it). God has provided for me and my kids with more than enough house. I get to live in the "quasi-country" too, so my place is replete with the sound of cows mooing from across the main road.

But show me a picture of a couple who has been married for twenty-five or more years, with all of their children and grandchildren playing in the local park, chasing butterflies and running with puppy dogs, and you might just find this girl sulking in a pool of her own tears. I wanted that picture for my own life—most "girls" do. But I didn't get it. Is it an unrealistic fantasy? Is real life like that? I suspect that behind every such scene, there is brokenness. Life is difficult. Nevertheless, I feel

My Will be Done

discontented, short changed, cheated, robbed and well?, down right envious. And I am not alone. If you happen to be struggling with envy right now—regardless of the object of that tension—let us consider it together. I believe there is hope for us. Acknowledgement is the first step.

The truth is that every family has issues. Some of the strongest couples I know are simply survivors of the same thing that caused my marriage to crumble. Alcoholism shook them violently, but did not break them. Adulterous affairs turned their worlds upside down, but they pushed through the incredible pain of those betrayals, forgave, repented and healed. Drug addiction, child suicide visited horror on some couples. Even though their stories are tales of triumph, the envy bug inside me looms large and I long to have had different outcomes in my life. I want what they have.

What do you do when you feel like breaking down, seeing a couple still holding hands after decades of marriage and looking at one another with knowing glances and battle tested love? If you are divorced, widowed or never been married, how do you respond when you attend social events or church functions and your family is the billboard for brokenness, or you simply attend alone?

The Word became flesh. And sometimes, that is right where I need the gospel to meet me: my flesh.

I turn to Joel 2:25-32 (NKJV):
So I will restore to you the years that the swarming
locust has eaten,
The crawling locust,
The consuming locust,
And the chewing locust
My great army which I sent among you.
²⁶ You shall eat in plenty and be satisfied,
And praise the name of the LORD *your God,*

> *Who has dealt wondrously with you;*
> *And My people shall never be put to shame.*
> *²⁷ Then you shall know that I am in the midst of Israel:*
> *I am the LORD your God*
> *And there is no other.*
> *My people shall never be put to shame.*

God cares whether we are shamed, because we are His. He knows our broken places because through Jesus, he entered them. Whether we are the cause of the explosions within our families, or the victims of them, He cares. And His caring is extended to us in a singular word: *restoration*. He says, "I will restore." We mortals may not know exactly the form that restoration will take. Our hope, and trust lies in that whatever has been lost, He will restore. I'm glad this verse does not say, "He *can* restore" or "He *might* restore." No, it affirms that He *will* restore." My confessional and honest prayer becomes,

> God, I don't how, when, nor where you will do it, but I
> choose to stand on Your promise to restore my loss.

These meditations remind me of a praise song we sing at my church that says, *"Whatever it sounds like, whatever it looks like, Come Lord Jesus."* We sometimes expect God to restore the way leading to our scripted outcome. We want it in neon lights, but He always shows up in ways that do not occur to me. I am reminded every single time He answers, that I am a speck, and that I must lay down my will and my expectations of His moving to restore. Only then am I able to set aside my envy and look into the perfect will of my Heavenly Father and say, "Not my will for restoration. But Yours alone."

What did your locusts destroy? What great opportunities were squandered by the generational loss to habitual sin in your heritage?

Restoration often involves repentance, but often, the "turning" may not come for years, even decades. Sometimes?

My Will be Done

Never. While you sit in the waiting on Him, He no doubt has a message for you. He may be calling you back to Himself in ways you never thought possible. My experience has shown me that real change does not come by compulsion, guilt, shame, or even fear of consequence. Please don't hear what I'm not saying. These feelings and emotions can lead to pierced hearts, which in turn lead to real change. But it is love for Him, gratefulness to Him, intimacy with Him that He wants for us.

"Love conquers all," they say. In God's economy, it happens to be true. Remember my song above, 'Whatever it looks like…Come."

So while we wrestle with wanting what others have, and what we think would be best for us, I close with this prayer:

> *Dear Lord,*
> *Thank You that You understand loss.*
> *And thank You for being our Restorer.*
> *We lay every loss at Your feet.*
> *We come with our envious hearts saying, Forgive us. We are Done with this destructive, ungrateful sin.*
> *We come in our brokenness begging, "Please heal; make us completely whole."*
> *But most of all, we forfeit our wills to say, "Whatever it looks like…Whatever it sounds like…Come, Lord Jesus. Just come."*
> *And we will be sure to give You the glory for it all.*
> *Honor Your Name in our lives.*
> *In Jesus Name.   Amen*

Sheri H. Thrower

Be done with being patient with everyone but you.
Be patient with yourself.

"Patience, dear."

1 Corinthians 13: 1 *"Love is patient..."*

My Will be Done

DONE

22 DONE WITH WRESTLING

One of my favorite childhood memories was going to my grandparent's home on Saturday mornings and watching my grandfather tune in to "The World Wide Wrestling Series." You would have thought that he was in the ring! I loved watching him perched on the edge of his brown leather recliner, leaning into the television set, huffing and puffing as he engaged in wrestling. He would swing with his left arm as if shadow boxing his opponent. Then, when one of the wrestlers body-slammed his opponent, the casual observer might have thought my grandfather had been slammed to the mat! He fought the "good fight," from his brown leather recliner!

Too often I find that I am engaged in worrisome matters that leave me flailing and exhausted in my recliner. Worry slams me into the corner, fear throws me across the ring. I fight and wrestle with what-ifs and "what might-have-beens." I argue with opinions and defend my case. The fight is real, but I am done wrestling—with flesh and blood, that is. I will never be done wrestling in the Spirit.

I have a friend who wrestled in the spirit daily over her daughter, who strayed from the ways of her upbringing and got pregnant out of wedlock. My friend entered the ring with the Devil, in full regalia. Now, every story does not turn out like this one, but she prayed her daughter back into fellowship with the Lord. She posted prayers and scriptures on her daughter's bedroom door each day. When her daughter was at work, my friend would go into her room and pray over her furniture, bed, walls, everything. She left nothing to chance, wrestling in the spirit for her child. The result? Her daughter is now happily married, involved in a local church with fully restored relationships with her mom and the Lord. There is power when a woman wrestles in the spirit.

My Will be Done

God's Word speaks to this: "*¹² For we wrestle not against flesh and blood, but against principalities, against powers, against the rulers of the darkness of this world, against spiritual wickedness in high places.*" Eph. 6: 12 (KJV)

This is no junior high wrestling match: principalities, powers, and rulers of darkness of this world. Add spiritual wickedness in high places. The war, as Christians know, has been won; thus, the Kingdom is here but not fully. Satan, after all, was given the Earth and he is still fighting to destroy as many as he can take with him. The battle rages on and we wonder why our prayers are hindered and delayed. Just look at our Enemy! He is not red, does not have a tail, and needs no pitch fork. He is adorned as an angel of light, masquerading around as something good. But only lies and deceit flow from him. He has nothing to offer but destruction.

We place a few toes into the ring of faith and along comes discord and dissension to discourage us. We find ourselves slammed to the ground. And as soon as we try to get up and fight again, the powers and rulers of darkness blindside us, place us in a "Full Nelson" of confusion and doubt. Spiritual wickedness in spiritual realms is layered above it all, and before we know it, we're pinned!

But scripture tells us in 1 John 4:4:, "...*Greater is He that is in you, than he that is in the world.*" (KJV). And so, just when we are exhausted from the struggle, along comes the Holy Spirit, our Comforter. In the Spirit, we get second wind, stand on our feet of faith and continue the fight to victory.

And herein lies our victory, when we recall the scripture: "So he answered me, "This is the word of the LORD to Zerubbabel: *'Not by strength or by might, but by My Spirit,' says the LORD of Hosts.'* " Zechariah 4:6 (HCSB)

As a teacher in public education, I must often recall that the battle in the classroom is not against flesh and blood, but is a spiritual one: nonsensical policies, unjust treatment of educators, that parents now rule the education system and administrators operate from a fear of legal action rather than failing children. This is true for parents too. A real Enemy wants to devour our children, and our "upside-down" culture makes it easier for them to be drawn away. As a single woman in today's culture, my flesh and blood can surely be distracted from God's purposes if I allow it, but He refocuses and realigns me into the ring of His will.

Where does your battle lie?

Be mindful that you cannot see, with your eyes, the *real* battle.

Slam the fear of tomorrow against the ropes of your faith.

Bring your spiritual weight to bear in long overdue prayers for your family. Fight.

Wrap up doubt and confusion with the grip of God's Word.

Sling your discouraging Opponent across ring with your prayers and praises. Huff and puff if you must. But do not give up. Do not give in.

Be done wrestling yourself and others.

Wrestle in heavenly realms, on your hands and knees.

My Will be Done

DONE

23 DONE WITH WHITE KNUCKLES

I would love to survey women to find out how many could count at least five of their life's years as "white knuckle years." By this I mean years where they have clung too tightly to people, money, relationships or dreams.

I can think of a few for myself. I held on to people or things to the point where God had to rip them from my clutches—one, tight finger at a time.

Juxtapose the "ripping" required for stubborn souls like me against what I would label "a nobler insight into the heart of God" by missionary, Jim Elliot, who was one "character" in the love story between him and notable author, Elizabeth Elliot. Both were servants of God, called to the mission field. Jim was killed on a mission trip in 1956 in Eastern Ecuador. Years later, Elizabeth returned to be a missionary to the tribe members who killed her husband. It is a remarkable story.

Elizabeth had loved Jim for years as they co-labored for the Lord, but she never told him. When their friendship blossomed into deeper intimacy, Jim told her (in a paraphrased form): "I must let you go. I must be as Abraham, laying my Isaac on the altar of sacrifice. I must give that which I love most to God. That would be you. I have to set you free to see if He will take you from me, or give you back to me." He loosened his grip of love on Elizabeth. And so for a time after his proclamation, they were thousands of miles apart with no communication between them. But God brought them back together for a life of love and ministry together. And though Jim was killed on the mission field some years later—leaving her a widow—their story inspires me deeply and has moved me to be more sacrificial and servant-hearted, trusting God to let go.

I heard Elizabeth's story on Christian radio years ago and it made me ask myself, "How willing am I to let go?" Am I

My Will be Done

willing to be done with my white knuckled grip on things or people whom I love? And what about my children, my parents, my sister and her family, career or ministry? How willing am I to lay these things or people on the altar of "letting go" before Christ? The truth is, as difficult as it may be, those things we love most must *remain* on that altar. As we trust them to Him, however, and walk away from that altar, we find His hand of provision sustaining those things within His will for us. And when He brings an end to those things not pleasing to Him, we learn to trust that every end is perfectly in His will for us, whether or not we see a perceived, better "replacement."

As parents, we know what "white knuckles" mean when it comes to raising our children. There comes that frightening moment—dare I say, especially for us moms—when they must leave us, despite our heart strings wrapped tightly around them. We let go one reluctant finger at a time. And as we see them make poor decisions—before or after they leave us—we wonder at the promise of Proverbs 22:6:

> *6 "Train up a child in the way he should go: and when he is old, he will not depart from it."* (KJV)

Ask the preacher whose son is on drugs, or his daughter who has become pregnant, out of wedlock… for the second time. Ask the most dedicated, Godly parent you perceive, "What happened?" Where does the "will not depart" become reality? Does it ever?

In the same way that most of us wandered off and were disobedient to parental instruction, our children go their own way, generally. It is part of the growing up process. Mistakes can be a tool to train us. But we do not always see it or feel that way when our kids are the ones being gossiped about.

As God's children, we have been doing it too. Just like the Israelites of the Old Testament, our hearts become hard at times, and we wander away. Does that mean our Heavenly Father is a "bad parent?" I think not. So as I ponder Proverbs 22, I find hope in the words, "...when he is old..." The Word planted in our children's hearts remains in them. We trust that the blossom comes when they are "old."

Loosen the grip and let God take hold.

Ladies? Do we hold on to the point of "control" of our men? Or, if single, have you "white knuckled" past relationships? As a teenager, I had a poster hanging in my room said that read, "If you love something, set it free. If it comes back, it is yours. If it doesn't it never was." I saw something "similar" on Facebook recently: "If you love someone, set them free. If they come back to you, no one else wanted them either." While I am certain the latter is meant to lend levity to the notion of "letting go" (and I did laugh!), it probably also serves to accentuate our culture's cynical view of commitment. In truth, the former seems right as we see demonstrated in the story of Abraham walking his son, Isaac up the mountain, out of obedience to the I Am That I Am.

In every situation...every circumstance...every time...

"Lord, do what only You can do."

Loosen our white-knuckle grips.

Lord, help me be done.

My Will be Done

Be done putting puny limitations
onto a limitless God.
He is unfathomable.

Unfathomable...

Isaiah 55:8 *"For my thoughts are not your thoughts, neither are your ways my ways," declares the Lord."* NIV

24 DONE WITH GREASED POLE THEOLOGY

Somewhere we got it all wrong. I would like to know who started the rumor that blessings slide down a slippery pole from heaven straight into our laps. Ask the biggest blessing receivers of all time, and they will tell you quite differently. Their blessings were not "greased pole blessings."

Take Abraham, for instance. He was promised a son, Isaac, who would be the beginning of an entire nation. With a promise like that from the Creator of the universe, it would seem a sure thing that all would fall into place. But there were obstacles between that promised blessing and the realization of it all. Abraham's wife laughed at the promise, took matters into her own hands and asked her won husband to sleep with their maidservant. Can you imagine? Sarah herself was ninety at the time. But these obstacles were just Sarah's manifested lack of faith.

For his part, Abraham was no spring chicken.. Despite the waiting and the strife and pain caused by the resulting child, Ishmael (to all involved), Isaac arrived. And from the "founding father's family dysfunction" right up to Joshua's small band of investigators viewing the giants in the Promised Land, there was struggle receiving God's blessing. And it is no different for us.

Another case in point? Jesus's mother, Mary. Her blessing "required" that all males under the age of two be murdered, that she and her family escape to Egypt until the threat had passed. But that was all after she gave birth to Savior in a cave, or an animal trough. Blessings don't come easy.

So why do we think our blessings should come without faith, a price, a sacrifice?

Blessings are much like the birth of a baby. They start out being a seed of promise and indescribable joy. Then, they need nourishment and a safe place to grow. Pretty soon, it is time for

My Will be Done

delivery. But with this stage comes all manner of pain, strife and yes, a little fear of the unknown. All this too, is washed away once the miracle arrives. And with each blessing, the work begins. What we perceive as God's blessings, at times, requires attention and devotion. A new house owns us, when we believe we own it. Possessions all decay. Raising children is one of the greatest labors we can experience on earth, but work is necessary: sleepless nights, concern for safety, broken hearts, and on and on. The blessings that last, however, are the spiritual ones we receive.

After waiting another forty years for a generation of the chosen people to die off in the wilderness, Joshua was poised finally to enter into God's Promised Land. And then? Jericho. Say what?! March around this obstacle for seven days doing what? Blowing musical instruments? Collective shouting? Just another "faith test"—or, perceived obstacle. Sometimes we just don't know. Our job is to press forward.

I have finally come to the realization in my fifties that I am going to simply expect conflict, especially when it comes to God answering prayer. It seems like clockwork: we pray, He hears and one of a number of answers to our prayer returns. Yes, no, or wait. Regardless of which, we manage to either imagine or experience trouble. But we should not be surprised by this, right? Jesus tells us to we will have trouble in this life. And whether in answer to a prayer, or receipt of a blessing, we can and do—at times—experience conflict. It is the world that tells us trouble is "bad." And we are so good at believing the lie aren't we? In God's economy, however, trouble is assured. And our growth in Him can explode in the middle of our trials, even though we are tempted to give up. It takes time for newborns to arrive, and to my knowledge, they never come with one push. Blessings in the form of answered prayers are no different.
Push.

Sheri H. Thrower

If you are "pushing through" in your prayer life today, waiting for an answer and expecting a blessing, contemplate God's word says in Isaiah 40:29-31 (Amplified version)

> "He gives strength to the weary,
> And to him who has no might He
> increases power.
> ^{30} Even youths grow weary and
> tired,
> And vigorous young men stumble
> badly,
> ^{31} But those who wait for the LORD
> [who expect, look for, and hope in
> Him]
> Will gain new strength and renew
> their power;
> They will lift up their wings [and
> rise up close to God] like eagles
> [rising toward the sun];
> They will run and not become
> weary,
> They will walk and not grow
> tired. "

I love the humanity displayed in these verses. It is honest and right to say that we are weary, that we are spent, that we stumble—and do so *badly*. But in the "but," we find the promise: But if we wait for the Lord, expect, look for, hope in Him, we see find promise of strength and renewal fulfilled.

There is no conduit from Heaven. Overnight deliveries are within His power, and do come from time to time, but those deliveries are the exception, and they generally will not grow our faith,

> Your blessing is on the way.
> Keep pushing.

My Will be Done

DONE

25 WELL, DONE

A friend sent me a picture the other night, by text, of his steak dinner. I responded with, "that cow is still mooing." Some people like their steaks barely warmed and that is their choice. I prefer mine a little more ...well..." "done"

It is my desire and prayer that after reading this book, you find yourself looking at a few areas of your life and asking, "Am I truly done with that?" Ask God to bring to mind the things in your life that need to end. Shut it down.

When it comes to your past, I hope you can say, "I am done." I do not dismiss the extent to which our pasts shape us, or even the unhealthy patterns that linger from events and traumas now decades past. But have we changed, matured, and left those behind? God promises to finish the work he started in each of us. But is our disobedience to what we know is "right" by His measure thwarting what He can do with us? I hope that with "I am done with my past," you are a set free blossom.

If you are a young person reading this (what is young you ask? Well, I'm fifty-one, so anyone younger than me!), be diligent about walking in obedience early in your life so that you may live longer in God's will. Remember: obedience is directly correlated to blessing. I am not talking here about a "works theology," by which I mean something like, "I will enter Heaven because I am a good person; or if I go to church, attend bible study, pray every day, and look the part, God is sure to bless me down here," all the while ignoring the precepts of His law—both Old and New. We will always live loved by God, but living *blessed* comes with obedience to His call through the Holy Spirit.

If you are like me, mid-life (or a little past mid!) and looking back, take a gander in your rearview mirror and recall:

Obedience is key to blessing. It is never too late to ask God to bring to mind those things that He wishes for you to be done with in your life. Christ was our great sacrifice. To be like Him means we, too, will sacrifice things and relationships (really, anything that has become an idol) in our lives to follow Him. If your grip has been tightly holding to the familiar, let this be the touchstone wherein you release your fingers—one at a time. Ask Him to help you let go. If there is a relationship or even a job you need wish farewell, then do so. Blessing is on the other side of your goodbye.

Whoever you are or wherever you are in life, God's will should reign supreme. Take a step back from being forehead to forehead with another, fists clenched, and move into His presence, today. Throw up your white flag of "my way" and tell Him, "Whatever it looks like, whatever it sounds like…come Lord, Jesus."

Finally, when you consider being done with "your way," what or who comes to mind? I bet you know the answer. You have simply been allowing it set up shop in your life. The thing or person has become familiar, a companion. Friend, if the Spirit is clearly showing you a person or situation to leave behind, tell Him about it now. Tell Him that you see that picture before you. Confess that it has been before Jesus's face long before it was before yours. Just as Abraham had to see his son Isaac on the altar of sacrifice, lay that image on the altar of your obedience and do the same saying, "Here, Lord. It is yours. I give it to you for you to take. Shape my will, my plan, my way. I want simply to be obedient to you." Friend? God will either take it or He will give it back. But He will do neither until we sacrifice everything to Him.

Everything.

Have you released it all? If you have, you will hear Him say the words that He said to His only Son, Jesus, "Well done, thou good and faithful servant." It will be confirmed in you.

And with this closing sentiments, my task of writing this book is done. I pray that God has moved and will continue to move in ways that only He can, through His word and His testimony through me.

And so it is with this seed or water, I leave the increase to Him, whether to encourage, convict, or inspire. He is the One with the power to change hearts and lives. And He is the true and Authentic Author of us all.

And I humbly conclude that I am…
Well,

Done.

"Our Father which art in Heaven,

Hallowed by Thy Name

Thy Kingdom Come

Thy Will Be Done on Earth as it is

in Heaven."

Contact Sheri

To contact Sheri for speaking or singing engagements, use the following:
Website: www.singakadamie.com
Facebook : Facebook.com/sheriproductions
Phone: 423.718.3647
Mail: P.O. Box 804 Ringgold, Ga. 30736

Made in the USA
Columbia, SC
09 August 2017